Sight Singing

Earl Henry
Webster University

PRENTICE HALL, Upper Saddle River, New Jersey 07458

Library of Congress Cataloging-in-Publication Data

HENRY, EARL.
　Sight singing / Earl Henry.
　　p.　cm.
　Includes index.
　ISBN 0-13-121336-9
　1. Sight-singing.　I. Title.
MT870.H46　1997
783'.0423—dc20　　　96-33609

Acquisitions editor: *Norwell Therien*
Production editor: *Edie Riker*
Cover design: *Kiwi Design*
Editorial director: *Charlyce Jones Owen*
Buyer: *Robert Anderson*

This book was set in 10.5/12 Baskerville by Thompson Type;
music was set by Music Publication Technologies; and it
was printed and bound by RR Donnelly & Sons Company.
The cover was printed by Phoenix Color Corp.

Credits and copyright acknowledgments appear on page 363
which constitutes an extension of the copyright page.

 ©1997 by Prentice-Hall, Inc.
Simon & Schuster / A Viacom Company
Upper Saddle River, New Jersey 07458

Printed in the United States of America

10　9　8　7　6　5　4　3　2　1

ISBN　　0-13-121336-9

Prentice-Hall International (UK) Limited, *London*
Prentice-Hall of Australia Pty. Limited, *Sydney*
Prentice-Hall Canada Inc., *Toronto*
Prentice-Hall Hispanoamericana, S.A., *Mexico*
Prentice-Hall of India Private Limited, *New Delhi*
Prentice-Hall of Japan, Inc., *Tokyo*
Simon & Schuster Asia Pte. Ltd., *Singapore*
Editora Prentice-Hall do Brasil, Ltda., *Rio de Janeiro*

for
Christine

Contents

Preface

While some authorities believe that students in musicianship classes must inevitably "sink or swim" based on innate abilities, *Sight Singing* is a workbook for creative learning and is grounded upon the philosophy that musicianship skills such as rhythmic reading and solfège can be taught and learned through progressive exercises and explanatory prose. Further, the text is in the form of a workbook so that students can acquire the skills necessary for success through a combination of class drill and individual practice outside class.

The twenty chapters of *Sight Singing* are broken into nine Units. Each Unit begins with a composition or excerpt that incorporates rhythmic, melodic, and harmonic problems to be discussed in the two or three chapters that follow. Students are not expected to perform these Unit Compositions until all chapters in a given Unit have been covered.

Sight Singing is not a theory text, yet because a comprehension of rhythmic, melodic, and harmonic materials is crucial in performance (especially at sight), many theoretical subjects (scales, meter, and chord progressions, for example) are discussed briefly. Still, each chapter begins with a list of **Allied Theoretical Concepts** that specify aspects of music theory that should be thoroughly understood *before the chapter is begun.*

Topics in both pitch and rhythm unfold progressively from the first to the last chapters. Aside from the Preliminary Studies, each chapter centers on five different areas: Warm-Ups, Exercises for Analysis or Composition, Studies, Excerpts from the Literature, and Ensembles. Each of these areas serves a different purpose and each is important for success in musicianship.

Warm-Ups. The passages identified as WARM-UPS are brief, but each incorporates a single rhythmic problem without pitch content, or one melodic problem with constant rhythmic values. The Warm-Ups are intended as exercises that might begin a class or individual practice period. Performance should be slow at first, but a balance between speed and accuracy is the ultimate goal.

Exercises for Analysis/Composition. Each chapter has an EXERCISE in either analysis or composition. Instructions in the text direct students either to analyze some aspect of an Exercise or to use one of the Exercises as a model for an original composition or variation. The Exercises do not include performance instructions (tempo, dynamics, phrasing, and so on). When students add these performance guidelines in French, German, Italian, or English (as directed), the Exercises will then constitute additional complete rhythmic reading and sight singing resources.

Studies.   Material in the text identified as STUDIES are complete, newly composed melodies for analysis, performance at sight, and/or practice on a particular melodic or rhythmic problem. The Studies focus on a specific area of performance with more repetition and in more detail than would be found normally in similar music from the traditional literature. Studies differ from the Exercises in that the former include tempo, dynamic, and expression marks in a variety of languages. In addition, many of the Studies are longer and generally more complete than the Exercises.

Excerpts from the Literature.   To balance the focused and repetitious nature of the Studies, each chapter includes several EXCERPTS FROM THE LITERATURE—passages from traditional Western music ranging in style from the Renaissance to the present day. These Excerpts demonstrate how composers of various eras used selected musical materials to create works of art. While most of the Excerpts were conceived originally for vocal performance, a few lyric melodies from instrumental music literature are included as well.

Ensembles.   Singing in ENSEMBLE poses problems that are quite different from those encountered in solo performance. Accordingly, each chapter closes with several Ensembles in two, three, or four parts. These Ensembles further reinforce rhythmic and pitch problems encountered in the chapter. Most of the Ensemble material comes from traditional Western music literature, but some have been newly composed specifically for this text by a number of different contemporary composers.

While music from the literature in this text is usually a complete phrase or group of phrases, the excerpts are often sections of longer compositions. Consequently, editorial changes were made when necessary:

1. If indications of tempo, dynamics, and phrasing were missing or minimal, they have been added or expanded to conform to the directions of the newly composed Studies.
2. The text has been omitted from vocal compositions in all cases.
3. Beaming has been changed from vocal style (a flag for each new syllable) to an instrumental notation (beams for complete beats and groups of beats).
4. The rhythmic values in final measures were altered where necessary to complete the measure. Likewise, an incomplete measure that begins an excerpt was renotated as an anacrusis.
5. Finally, if more than one measure of rest appeared in the original, the music has been renotated as a single measure of rest with a fermata.

ACKNOWLEDGEMENTS

I am pleased to acknowledge the help of several individuals in the preparation of this book. First, I want to thank Dr. James Mobberley and Dr. James Greeson of the Universities of Missouri (Kansas City) and Arkansas (Fayetteville) respectively. These noted composers kindly took time to write original works that I used in this text as "Unit Compositions."

Edie Riker supervised the production of this text for Prentice Hall. Her design and editorial suggestions are much appreciated. Likewise, Carl Simpson's meticulous efforts as music editor were of considerable value. Finally, I am truly grateful to Dr. Michael Rogers of the University of Oklahoma (Norman). Dr. Rogers read the manuscript in its early stages and provided not only the exceptional foreword that follows, but many suggestions that allowed me to define my work more sharply. I recommend that students begin their work by reading Dr. Rogers' elegant foreword, then refer often, during subsequent studies, to his knowledgeable assessment of problems and procedures in sight singing and rhythmic reading.

Earl Henry
St. Louis, Missouri

Foreword

Teaching aural skills in music theory traditionally involves focus on both dictation and sight singing. These two activities are simply different avenues to the single goal of developing internal musical perception—the ability to hear musical relationships accurately and with understanding. It would be difficult to imagine two activities more intertwined or mutually reinforcing than these.

The purpose of dictation, for example, is to produce not correct written transcriptions but a certain kind of listener who can hear sound as meaningful patterns. Likewise, the purpose of sight singing is not to provide a sight-reading service for music department choral groups or to develop articulate vocal response, although these may be worthwhile fringe benefits. The goal, again, is to produce a listener who can hear musical patterns. The final step of externalizing one's hearing through notation or sung performance is useful for checking accomplishment and providing teaching feedback, but it is not an inherent part of the activity itself. The sound-into-notes and notes-into-sound transference could be aptly described as developing the understanding ear and hearing mind.

Skill in being able to imagine and hear music inside one's head from a printed score, which is the real goal of sight singing, is considered by many teachers, however, to be even more basic than the reverse process of writing down notes from played examples as in dictation. In fact, it would be difficult to imagine an activity that contributes more to the development of mature musicianship than sight singing. There is something especially powerful about conjuring sounds out of one's personal stockpile of stored memories and experiences that exceeds the more passive activity of responding to patterns already provided by an external source.

The term "sight singing" is itself a misnomer. Practiced and imagined in the proper way, the activity is not actually something learned over again each time a new melody is performed. Approached correctly, the task of singing a previously unseen example "at sight" translates into the task of understanding more-or-less common features in the tune at hand as compared with the dozens or hundreds of previously viewed examples. The very characteristics that identify a melody as tonal, for example, will ensure that practiced examples share joint properties of structure and organization with newly tested material. Viewed in this way, sight singing becomes more like pattern recognition. Any melody that is likely to appear on an exam will contain figures and designs encountered already many times before in the practice room or class.

In a sense, then, an important goal of the sight-singing class is to enculturate the student into the world of various pitch (and durational) systems. In this regard, the sight-singing class often involves—or should involve—an analysis component focusing on how melodies are put together and how given exercises might be variations or exemplars of more basic archetypes. Taught in this way, sight singing is not a separate or extra topic in the curriculum but reinforces—and is reinforced by—many other topics that deal with typical pitch languages, including harmony and form. Once this particular approach is taken seriously, the task at hand becomes greatly simplified from both the teacher's and student's perspective, and the secondary goal can begin, of convincing the student how "easy" it is to do sight singing—that is, how easy it is to recognize patterns that have already been seen, heard, assimilated, and performed many times over (but perhaps with the changed garb of clef, key, rhythm, meter, tempo, style, etc.). In short, the *ear* training that results from sight-singing practice is really channeled by *mind* training.

Another aspect of the misnomer label involves the actual medium of performance—i.e., the act of singing itself. Focus can sometimes be redirected away from singing (with the fringe benefit of lessening student fear and embarrassment) by concentrating instead on the skill of "inner hearing" (the internal mental processing of musical relationships), which is what sight-singing practice is intended to improve. The audible performance of the melody is simply the by-product of the audiated image and is necessary, obviously, for evaluation purposes, but not as an end in itself. Sight singing is not done primarily to refine *oral* production but rather to strengthen the imagination for conceiving and conceptualizing *aural* patterns.

One of the most convenient aspects of practicing sight singing is that it can be done so easily outside of class, although certainly time should also be spent in the classroom to help students know what they should concentrate on during their individual sessions. The following will provide some practical tips:

a. All students should become totally familiar with the individual nooks and crannies of their own range: e.g., the highest and lowest pitches they can sing comfortably; the easiest keys to sing in (both when tonic is at the extremes of the tonality frame and when tonic is positioned in the middle); the conditions under which falsetto may be required; the "bad" notes for their voice, etcetera.

b. brief, *but frequent,* practice sessions are far more beneficial than marathon sessions done once or twice a week. Even just five or ten minutes a day (this means *every* day, seven days a week) is far better than two hours the night before the weekly test. The rule of thumb is "short doses repeated often." In addition, practicing is something that needs to be scheduled into the daily routine, like homework or ensemble rehearsals, or brushing one's teeth. Relegating practicing (or doing homework) to spare time or leftover slots usually means it will not be done at all, since most college students have no spare time.

c. when working in the practice room, the student should pretend that the performance is "for real" (i.e., for an audience or teacher) and, conversely, when performing on an exam, that one is "just practicing" (i.e., making no "big deal" about it). The idea ultimately is to downplay the difference between practicing and performing; it is all just one thing—making music. Such an attitude could profitably carry over into actual recital preparation and training for all public performance events. What a novel idea that sight-singing practice could be related to something in the real world!

d. the "buddy system" (working with a friend or classmate), which is commonly used for dictation practice (playing melodies for one another), can also be used for sight-singing rehearsal. The idea is to alternate the role of teacher and student in working through practice material. Recognition of the strengths and weaknesses of peers can sensitize one's own awareness and be an early step toward improving one's own performance level.

e. silent singing both in class and privately is an excellent approach for strengthening the inner hearing skill mentioned above.

f. recording one's performance (any simple cassette player will do) with subsequent self-evaluation is invaluable for diagnosis and progress.

g. practicing many different melodies in a single tonality for a period of fifteen or twenty minutes can often be an effective way of instilling tonal bearings (the sense of knowing, at any given moment, where one is located in the key in relation to selected reference notes). Eventually the typical key-defining patterns begin to stand out with stark clarity, as grooves of familiarity are etched into one's memory banks. Tonality begins to drip from the walls after practicing in any single key for an extended time; tonic hangs in the air like a tangible presence. The goal of sight singing is suddenly and palpably revealed not as "how to sing the next note," but as learning a large and intricate, yet beautifully simple, framework for hearing.

h. when practicing with a piano (or any reference instrument), the keyboard can, of course, be useful for giving a starting pitch, but the urge to pound out the answer or problem notes on the piano should be strenuously resisted. A rule of playing only tonic (or at the most, only tonic/dominant) should be strictly enforced. When faced with a problem passage or troublesome note, the students should remind themselves of where the tonic or dominant pitch lies—even though it might not be the next pitch—in order to seek a proper orientation. It's best if this reminder can come from the internalized memory of the music's tonality rather than from striking the piano. Often just noticing where the troublesome note is moving to (rather than where it is coming from) or simply singing aloud (or remembering) one of the tonic triad triad pitches as a reference will suffice, since none of the twelve chromatic pitches is more than a step away from some point on the tonic-triad grid.

The secret to singing the "difficult" notes is to know precisely where the simple ones are located. Understood in this way, no pitches are truly difficult. Eventually, as students become acclimated to all the props of the tonal scaffolding, they can be weaned from playing anything on the piano. The art of sight singing at this level becomes just a simple act of fitting the pitches of a given melody directly into an omnipresent, aurally imagined, tonal blueprint spread before the ears—a blueprint that the skillful teacher will help bring into the sharpest focus at every opportunity. It is learning this generic blueprint of tonality itself, as much as the particular details of particular melodies, that makes for successful pedagogy.

It is absolutely essential to use some kind of organized routine for examining and performing a melody at testing time—a routine that eventually becomes ingrained and automatic through repetition and habit. Presumably, students will rehearse with this same routine as part of their practice sessions, so all of the suggestions included below are really just further elaborations of the previous tips.

Many kinds of organized routines are possible and useful. Thoughtful students (and thoughtful teachers) will eventually evolve an individualized set of procedures. The one I recommend as a sample—at least to start with—is an adaptation of a plan favored by Gary Potter (Indiana University). At first it may seem tedious, cumbersome, and time consuming, but with practice the steps can become swiftly blended and fluidly realized by second nature. There is definite merit, however, when first learning how to sight sing, in breaking down the procedure into discrete steps, especially for diagnosis of problem areas when things go wrong.

1. ANALYZE the given tune: key/scale; meter/tempo; phrases/cadences; recurring motifs; key-defining pitches vs. decorative pitches; high/low points; tonality frame (relative positioning within the range of the tonic/dominant axis); harmonic implications and chord outlines; contour (skips vs. steps); sequences and other repetitions; contrasting vs. parallel organization; formal layout; archetypal patterns; long-range step progressions (internalized scales); etc. Noting such details will be a real chore at first. This is why good sight singing requires such a heavy dose of classroom melodic analysis practice. [In some classes more time might be spent doing this type of analysis than in actually singing.]

The eventual goal is to preview the melody visually by rapidly scanning for both stereotypical patterns (common to many tunes—especially ones previously encountered) and distinctive features that make this particular melody special, unique, idiosyncratic, or problematic.

2. ORIENT to the key: tonal grounding for the mind's ear and for the physical formation of sound (i.e., experiencing the specific key in the muscles of vocal production—or even getting them to vibrate at all). This is accomplished through some kind of quick vocal (and mental) warm-up using: a) a sim-

ple arpeggio of the tonic triad; b) singing up and down the scale; c) a simple outline of a predetermined cadence pattern; or d) some other preliminary key-defining tonal formula worked out in advance in consultation with the teacher.

Unlike the first step above, this second phase is aural, not visual.

3. SILENT SING (in the actual key determined above) the melody, noting trouble spots.

4. Finally, after all the preceding steps, SING the melody ALOUD. This is the "first reading."

5. Mentally EVALUATE the result: further "figuring out the solution," i.e., comparing the sung version (step 4) with the imagined correct version (step 3). This is the "second analysis."

6. SING AGAIN: the "second reading" (a corrected version and the final graded "answer").

Genuine improvement in sight singing cannot be gained through a simplistic drill-and-repetition format of instruction—although the benefits of rigorous and regular practice certainly should not be underestimated. Besides having an organized routine for performing (as outlined above), for maximum impact some conceptual framework must be part of the student's training and thinking as well. Five methods are offered below as possibilities. A shorter (or longer) list could just as easily be constructed, but most approaches or methodologies would end up being variations or combinations of the following:

Intervallic.   This is probably the most commonly used approach (partly because individual interval identification often makes up an early and large part of aural-skills programs), but is not without its problems. There certainly are situations where finding correct pitches through reference to interval distances can be helpful, but in general, learning to hear in such a mechanical note-to-note way is inherently unmusical, as important longer-range threads of structural connection are ignored. At the least, this method should be bolstered with other approaches.

In addition, the problem of changing psychological effect (and affect) according to context cannot be discounted. For example, the "Twinkle Twinkle Little Star" sound of the opening P5 is only valid for situations where tonic and dominant pitches (scale degrees 1–5) are activated. But there are five other locations just within the diatonic major scale (2–6, 3–7, 4–1, etc.) where other P5 pairings are also found—each with its distinctive flavor of inherent tensions or stabilities and different experiential "feel"—and all are either subtly or grossly unlike the "Twinkle" case. Another example: the minor third as heard between tonic and minor mediant (1–♭3) is a completely different sensation than the same distance as measured by the augmented second found within a harmonic minor scale (♭6–♯7)—likewise with dozens of other examples.

Harmonic.   This approach can be useful when attention to chord outlines, arpeggiations, or implied progressions is desired.

Structural Reductions.   Melodies can often be profitably studied in skeletal form to reveal their essential underpinnings by skimming off embellishing pitches, repeated notes, etc. The point is not that some notes are important while others are not, but rather that some notes give meaning while others are dependent for their meaning on more foundational tonal reinforcers, just as a building or bridge is supported by various structural arrangements of girders, pillars, and cross beams.

By representing or performing a complex melody (pitch and/or rhythm) in a simplified form, students can be led more easily to an accurate hearing and understanding of its organization and can be led more easily to comparisons between melodies that on the surface may seem different but in reality share underlying points of similarity. Embedded lines and buried scale patterns, for example, often become instantly recognizable in a simplified version. For the same reason, practicing themes with their corresponding variations side by side (or even simultaneously with a group!) can be vividly instructive. And highly chromatic examples can be compared with their less intense diatonic counterparts.

Once structural pitches are defined and clearly established in the mind's ear, the more decorative layers of the foreground can be added back in one at a time. What at first seemed overwhelmingly intricate can turn out to be commonplace, as the placement of individual events is seen, heard, and understood in relation to the whole—a whole, by the way, that likely will have been experienced many times before. Structural reductions are commonly produced in the analysis class but what I am recommending here is that they be sung as well.

Solfège Systems.   The application of syllables to represent location within a key has traditionally been of benefit to many students. The long-standing controversies and pros and cons of the various competing systems—or whether even to use syllables at all—are too complex to discuss in this short essay, but three possibilities can at least be mentioned: 1) fixed "do" (generally of greater value for learning to read music than for hearing relationships within a key); 2) movable "do/la"-based minor ("do" is always tonic for each major key, with the relative minor borrowing the same syllables, sometimes called the Kodály system and useful for modal and folk-song literature); and 3) movable "do/do"-based minor (syllables for minor derived from the parallel major: resulting in "do" being used for tonic in both major and minor keys). This last system is currently in greatest use nationally at the college level and is believed by many leading authorities to best project the internal relationships found in tonal music. Scale-degree numbers would be yet an additional variation of this scheme, although they do not easily permit distinctions of sound or function within chromatically altered situations. Using letter names, on the other hand, would correspond in effect to fixed "do."

Scale-Degree Function.   This approach agrees conceptually with option 3 ("do"-based major and minor) mentioned above and stresses learning the tendency-tone and resolution patterns that operate in defining the pitch centricity found in the major/minor tonal system of the common-practice period. The foundation of this method rests on the internal tugs, pulls, and proclivities that pitches exhibit for one another in tonal settings. In fact, it is this total network of magnetic attractions that defines functional tonality, including relationships found not only in melodic structures but in harmonic progressions too. Scale-degree attractions such as 7–1, 4–3, 2–1, 5–1, 6–5, etc. are some of the common pairings found in this system.

Most teachers will favor some combination of approaches—as much for variety as from conviction or simply for complementary ways of solving problems. The remarkable book that follows will provide a cornucopia of exercises, warm-ups, analyses, rhythms, ways of activating the suggestions made above, additional suggestions of its own, and, of course, hundreds of creative and supple melodies. This book is clearly much more than the typical anthology of practice tunes. The amount of textbook prose is unusually high for a sight-singing book; this shows the author's unmistakable commitment to actually explaining the "how and why" of sight singing as opposed to merely constructing another collection of material for performance. It is a highly ambitious and richly imagined text—a total musicianship approach that is expertly designed and paced.

There are no shortcuts for learning to sight sing. Progress is always the result of hard work and a clearly organized and interesting course of study. This book defines the true core of the subject—not the "tricks of the trade," but the trade itself.

Michael R. Rogers
University of Oklahoma

DIATONIC PATTERNS

James Mobberley, Étude

ÉTUDE means "study" in French and is usually a composition that centers on a specific problem in musical performance. The term is especially associated with Frédéric Chopin (1810–49), who wrote many such compositions for piano. Composers of études usually strive to create works of serious artistic merit, while at the same time including the repetition necessary to master a given aspect of vocal or instrumental technique. In Mobberley's composition, stepwise and gapped-scale patterns as well as simple meters are under "study."

JAMES MOBBERLEY,[1] *ÉTUDE*

[1]James Mobberley (b. 1954) is a professor on the composition faculty of the Conservatory of Music at the University of Missouri—Kansas City. He has received numerous fellowships, grants, and awards including a Guggenheim Fellowship, the Rome Prize Fellowship, and many others. His music spans many media including orchestra, film, and chamber music. Dr. Mobberley has been interested in music that combines electronic and computer music with live performance.

IN UNIT ONE

For those who have little or no experience in sight singing and rhythmic reading, Chapter 1 consists of preliminary studies in several of the basic intervals of our musical system: the half step, the whole step, the octave, and the unison. You will notice that with the exception of measures 6, 7, and 13 in *Étude,* all intervals are either half or whole steps. You will also discover that the element of time in Western music is based upon a continuous pulse known as the *beat.* The beats are organized into patterns of strong and weak pulses called *meter.* Finally, Chapter 1 includes a variety of terms and symbols that govern *nuance*—the more sensitive aspects of musical performance.

When you listen to and perform Mobberley's *Étude,* you should be aware that E♭ is the most important pitch. This is the effect of *tonality* or *key,* which establishes one pitch as more important than the others. The composer created this effect carefully through a variety of means. In Chapter 2, you will learn about melodic cadences—formulas that conclude phrases (measures 4, 8, 12, and 16 of *Étude*). You will find that some pitches are relatively stable and that others have strong tendencies to move or resolve. Your studies will include concepts such as melodic range and contour, and you will learn as well that composers use such forms and techniques to create stability and contrast. Finally, you will study the *major scale,* through which many traditional melodies are organized.

CHAPTER ONE

Preliminary Melodic Exercises
The Beat and Rhythmic Notation

Allied Theoretical Concepts
- The Keyboard and Basic Pitch Notation
- The Octave
- Half and Whole Steps
- Notational Symbols for the Beat

Concepts in Pitch: Singing Whole and Half Steps

Traditional Western music is based on the OCTAVE—a natural duplication of pitch indicated by two notes that have the same letter name. The pitches C, below, are an octave apart.

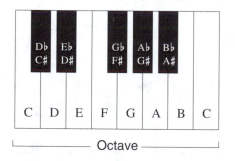

A HALF STEP is the distance from one key on the keyboard to the next closest key above or below. Notice on the diagram above that the octave is divided into twelve half steps. Two half steps combine to form a WHOLE STEP—another of the basic intervals in Western music. The interval between the pitches C and D in the diagram above is a whole step (comprised of two half steps). Finally, when two pitches are identical, the interval is termed a UNISON or PRIME.

Octave   Unison (Prime)   Half Steps   Whole Steps

When singing intervals and melodies, check your pitch often against the keyboard, but only after you have sung; otherwise, you are just learning to mimic. Use the piano to check, not to *find* the pitch. In singing tonal melodies, if you get lost and need some help, play not the troublesome pitch that is causing you difficulty, but the tonic (or sometimes the dominant) pitch of the scale.

Concepts in Rhythm and Meter: The Beat and Metric Patterns

Time is measured in terms of BEATS—the underlying pulse that makes us want to move in regular patterns with the music. A NOTE represents both the duration and the pitch of a musical tone.

Rests.   The symbols for silence are RESTS. Each note has a corresponding rest.

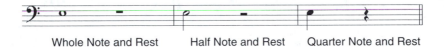

| Whole Note and Rest | Half Note and Rest | Quarter Note and Rest |

The Dot and Tie.   A DOT added to a note or rest increases the value by one-half. A TIE (♩‿♩) combines the value of two or more pitches. Both the dot and the tie create notes of longer duration.

1 beat   2 beats   3 beats   4 beats

Meter

When a regular pattern of strong and weak beats recurs, that pattern is called a METER. If the beat pattern is strong-weak (> ∪), for example, the meter is termed DUPLE; when the metric pattern is strong-weak-weak (> ∪ ∪) the meter is TRIPLE. QUADRUPLE METER features patterns of four beats. A complete metric pattern (whether duple, triple, or quadruple) is known as a MEASURE.

Counting.   Use the beat number ("one," "two," and so on) to count beat units. When notes of longer duration occur, continue singing the initial beat number without break. *Feel* (rather than articulate) the beat numbers in the case of rests and ties.

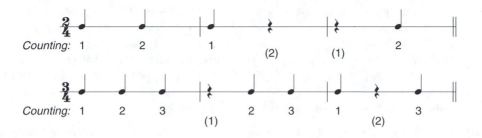

Conducting. Traditional conducting patterns will be useful when you perform music at sight. The first beat is always down; the last (the *anacrusis*) is upward. Other arm movements depend on the number of beats in the measure.

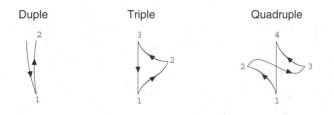

Anacrusis. Composers sometimes begin a work with an incomplete measure called an ANACRUSIS. The notes that complete the initial measure appear at the end of the composition. Rhythmic Study #1 and Melodic Study #3 in this chapter, for example, both begin with an anacrusis.

Interruptions in the Beat. Once a beat is established, composers sometimes interrupt it with special effects. The FERMATA (⌒) indicates that a note or rest is to be held long enough to break the prevailing pulse. A CAESURA (//) indicates a silence that likewise interrupts the beat flow. Finally, if the composer wants a silence to be especially significant, the letters G.P ("General Pause") may accompany a rest symbol and/or fermata.

PERFORMANCE INSTRUCTIONS

In addition to the notes themselves, composers usually include instructions regarding the manner of performance. These instructions include tempo and dynamics, articulation, and nuance—among others.

Tempo and Dynamics. The speed of the beat is called the TEMPO. One of the goals of this text is to familiarize you with the most important foreign terms for tempo. While you might indicate the speed of the beat in your own composition as "Moderate," a traditional composition by a Frenchman might be labeled *Modéré;* a German could use *Mässig;* and an Italian would designate the tempo as *Moderato.*

Degrees of loudness are called DYNAMICS. Composers indicate dynamic level mainly through a set of Italian terms and abbreviations such as *piano* ("soft") or *mezzoforte* ("moderately loud"). These terms are abbreviated *p* and *mf* respectively. Changes in dynamics are indicated simply by inserting a new term or abbreviation. Gradual changes in intensity are suggested through graphic symbols (⋖ and ⋗) or with words like *crescendo* ("increasing volume") or *decrescendo* ("diminishing in volume").

Expression.   Composers today generally give very specific instructions for the performance of their music. In addition to terms for tempo and dynamics, traditional composers often included instructions for EXPRESSION (nuance) such as *cantabile* (It. "singing"), *ruhig* (Gr. "calm"), or *gracieux* (Fr. "graceful"). These directions are essential to a faithful and musical performance of traditional works.

Glossary.   An extensive glossary of foreign terms and symbols is included in this text. The first time you encounter an unfamiliar term, just look it up! Most instructors, however, will require students to memorize the most important terms and symbols.

In music before about 1750, composers did not normally include tempo or dynamic instructions in their music. Accordingly, when you encounter these specific directions in earlier music, they are typically *editorial*— that is, added by someone other than the composer. Editorial indications in this text, as well as those in other publications, represent only one possible interpretation of a composer's music. If the indications were actually provided by the composer, of course (after about 1750), they should be given more weight.

RHYTHMIC READING

I. WARM-UPS

Use counting syllables to perform the following brief passages, which feature a variety of beat and multiple-beat patterns in simple meter. Conduct as you sing.

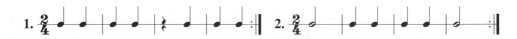

II. EXERCISES

Analysis.   Begin by adding tempo and performance instructions in English to the three rhythmic solos below. Prior to performance, study each solo and undertake an analysis of the rhythm and meter. Consider the following in your study of the music:

a. What is the basic metric pattern (duple, triple, and so on)?
b. How many different note values are used?
c. To what extent (if any) are rests used?
d. Are dots and ties used? If so, to what extent?
e. Do some patterns recur?

Composition.   Use one or more of the solos above as the basis of compositions of your own. Notate your music on a separate sheet and use the same meter, length, and so on, as the solo you choose as a model. Limit your rhythmic vocabulary to note values of one beat's duration or longer. Use dots and ties as appropriate.

Analyze the passages below, then perform them on a single pitch using counting syllables. Pay close attention to the tempo, dynamic, and other indications.

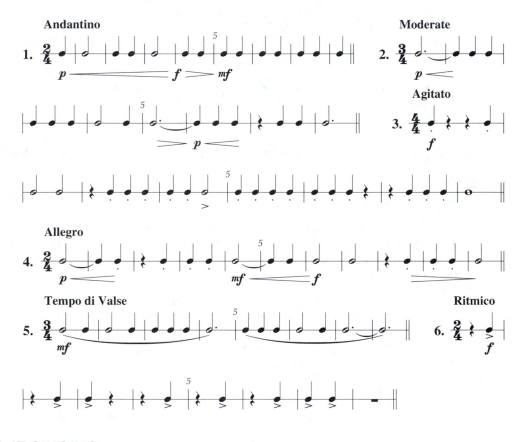

SIGHT SINGING

As early as A.D., 1000 musicians were devising and writing about methods to help singers perform unfamiliar music through SIGHT SINGING. One of these systems, called SOLFÈGE, will be studied in the next chapter. At present, however, your sight-singing exercises will be limited to whole steps, half steps, unisons, and octaves.

Using the Keyboard.   Most students will need to use the keyboard to find the first pitch of an exercise. Use the keyboard also to check pitch in your private practice and to find a comfortable octave. Make a habit of playing the final note of an exercise on the keyboard after you sing it to make sure that your performance was accurate.

I. WARM-UPS

A. Play each pitch below on the piano or another instrument.[2] Name each pitch before you sing it. Repeat the exercises, singing both the given pitch and an octave above or below it, as appropriate for your range.

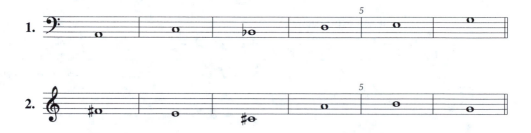

B. Repeat the exercises above to include a half or whole step above or below the given pitch. Play the first pitch on the keyboard, match that pitch, then sing the designated interval above or below before returning to the original pitch.

II. PRELIMINARY SIGHT-SINGING EXERCISES

The passages that follow consist of note and rest patterns using beat and multiple-beat units. These passages also include suggestions of tempo, dynamics, and expression. Use the glossary to look up any unfamiliar terms and pay close attention to the performance directions.

[2]Please note that some instruments, like the clarinet and trumpet, *sound* pitches different from those that they read on the score.

CHAPTER TWO

Major Scales
Simple Beat Division and Subdivision

Allied Theoretical Concepts
- Major Scales
- Melodic Cadences
- The Simple Beat Division and Subdivision

Concepts in Pitch: Major Scales

A SCALE is an organized series of pitches around which traditional melody is based. The descending series is the reverse of this pattern.

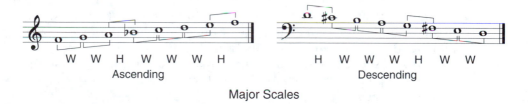

Ascending   Descending

Major Scales

Scale Degrees. The first pitch of a scale is the TONIC and is also the first scale degree (represented $\hat{1}$ in this text). A SCALE DEGREE is a number that shows the relationship between the tonic and another given pitch in the scale. Pitches included within a given scale are DIATONIC; pitches outside a scale are NONDIATONIC.

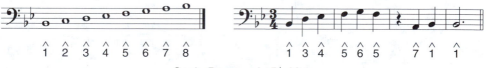

Scale Degrees in B♭ Major

MELODIC CADENCES

A PHRASE is a complete musical statement that can be either *terminal* or *progressive* depending upon which scale degree ends the phrase. This final (accented) pitch of a phrase constitutes the melodic *cadence*. A CADENCE is an ending formula that imparts either a feeling of completion (terminal) or division (progressive). Terminal melodic cadences typically end with $\hat{1}$ or $\hat{3}$ (measures 4, 12, and 16 of *Étude*). If a phrase is heard as incomplete (progressive), the last pitch will often be $\hat{5}$, $\hat{2}$, or $\hat{7}$ (measure 8, for example).

Motives.   Music is not typically THROUGH COMPOSED—that is, written from beginning to end without the repetition or variation of material. A MOTIVE is a minimal, but memorable series of two or more pitches. Notice that in *Étude* (pages 1–2) the two principal motives are bracketed; letters like *m* and *n* are often used to identify motives. The analysis of motives is essential in rhythmic reading and sight singing.

Variation.   While composers often simply repeat motives, altering a motive through VARIATION is another common compositional device. In analysis, the variant of a motive can be identified with an exponent. A variation of motive "m," for example, could be identified as "m^1"; a second variation of motive "n" would be labeled "n^2." Notice that motive "m" in measure 1 of *Étude* is inverted in measure 9 ("m^1"). Likewise, motive "n" in measure 3 is inverted in measure 11 ("n^1").

Sequence.   Motives that are varied through a series of ascending or descending statements (legs) are called SEQUENCE. Normally, three statements of the pattern are included in sequence, although one or more of them may be altered. Sequence can be a powerful force in the development of melody and should be identified in analysis. The first phrase below features ascending sequence; the second, descending. Notice that both cadences occur on strong beats.

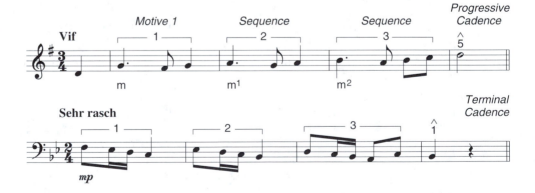

Concepts in Rhythm: Beat Division and Subdivision

When composers use smaller note values, they typically choose either to divide the beat into two or into three equal parts. The two-part division, known as SIMPLE, will be studied in the present chapter; the three-part or COMPOUND DIVISION is discussed in Chapters 3 and 4.

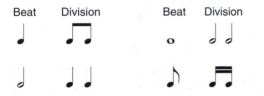

COUNTING THE BEAT DIVISION AND SUBDIVISION[1]

Counting syllables enhance rhythmic performance. Numbers like "one," "two," or "four" are used to count the beat itself. In simple meters, use the syllable "te" to perform the beat division. Remember that as long as the accent pattern and tempo remain the same, various note values can represent the beat and beat division.

Count silently if notes are held, or if there are rests.

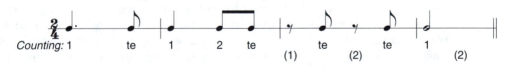

Subdivision.   When smaller note values are desired, the beat division itself can be SUBDIVIDED into two equal parts.

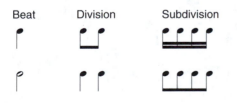

[1]The system of counting presented here is but one of many. Your instructor may prefer an alternate method.

The counting syllable "ta" may be used to enunciate the beat subdivision.

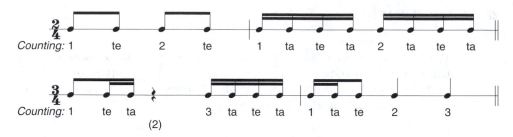

Counting: 1   te   2   te   1   ta   te   ta   2   ta   te   ta

Counting: 1   te   ta   (2)   3   ta   te   ta   1   ta   te   2   3

RHYTHMIC REDUCTION

Use rhythmic reduction to separate the problems of rhythmic performance from those of pitch. RHYTHMIC REDUCTION refers to the process of performing the rhythms of a composition but without the notated changes in pitch. Notice how the first phrase of *Étude* can be rewritten or visualized for rhythmic performance alone. Compare the reduction below to the beginning of the original on page 1.

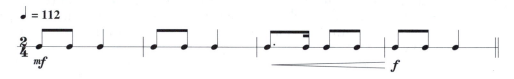

RHYTHMIC READING

I. WARM-UPS

The rhythmic warm-ups in this text are designed to be performed in two different ways. First, they may be sung on a single pitch using solfège syllables, counting syllables, pitch names, or scale-degree numbers. In addition, the warm-ups may be sung as scales—ascending the first time through, then descending on the repeat.

Warm-Up

Performed as Scale

10/5/15

Warm-Up

Performed as Scale

10/5/15

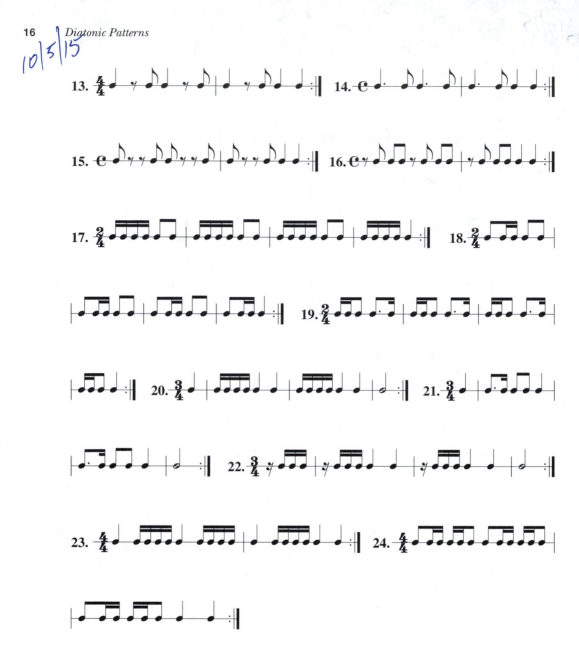

II. EXERCISES

Analysis. Study the three rhythmic solos that follow. First add tempo indications and performance instructions *in Italian*. Continue with a thorough rhythmic analysis.

2.

3. [music notation]

Composition.   Choose one or more of the solos above, and on a separate sheet, compose two different variations based on the original. Limit your rhythmic vocabulary to the materials that have been presented thus far. A true variation sounds similar to the original, yet is altered in some significant way. Consider the following as possible approaches to the first solo.

    a. Maintain the original tempo, but halve or double most note values of the original.

    b. Change the meter so that the original (long-short) relationships are recognizable, but quite different.

Original

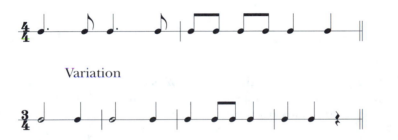

Variation

    c. Create stress on normally weak beats with dynamic accents.

    d. Replace selected notes in the original with rests in one or both of the variations.

    e. Contrast the variations with differing dynamics, articulations, and indications of expression.

SIGHT SINGING

I. WARM-UPS

    A.   Play the first pitch on the piano or another instrument, then use a syllable recommended by your instructor to match the pitch in a convenient octave. Name each pitch as you sing it.

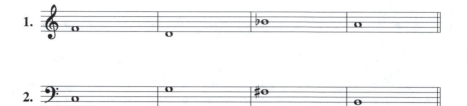

B. Scales.   Sing the following scales ascending and descending. Practice other major scales throughout your range as well.

C. Stepwise Patterns Within the Major Scale.   The passages below involve stepwise motion among the scale degrees in major. Identify melodic cadences and speculate on an appropriate tempo for each melody.

D. Gapped-Scale Patterns.   The following passages include stepwise motion within the major scale as well as leaps of major and minor thirds (a gap in the stepwise motion). First practice the complete scalar pattern including the cue-sized notes. Next, omit the cue notes to produce the gapped patterns.

E. Scale Degrees One and Five.   As you will learn in other chapters of this text, 1̂ and 5̂ are the most important degrees in a scale. Practice first in four- and five-pitch scalar patterns. Next, omit the intervening pitches and sing 1̂ to 5̂ as well as 5̂ to 1̂ (8̂), both ascending and descending.

II. EXERCISES

Study the melodies below. Prepare an analysis of one or more as directed by your instructor. Begin by adding any performance instructions *in Italian* that you feel add expression to the music.

Composition.   On a separate sheet, compose one or more melodies that feature characteristics similar to those above. You might use the same scale, for example, the same rhythm, the same phrase structure, and so on. Include tempo and performance indications in Italian (look these up in the glossary if necessary).

III. STUDIES

Before performing the studies for the first time, analyze them carefully as suggested by Mobberley's *Étude,* which can be found at the beginning of UNIT I. Set an appropriate tempo, then perform the study from beginning to end *without breaking the tempo.* If the passage proves difficult, isolate problematic measures and practice them more slowly. Consider performing the passage on a single pitch as a rhythmic study.

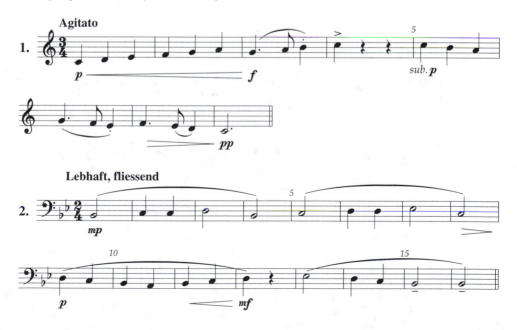

6.

cedèz

7. Maestoso   Più mosso

rallentando

8. ♩ = 120

accel.

9. Valse

10. ♩ = 120

a little faster

a tempo

IV. EXCERPTS FROM THE LITERATURE

GIOVANNI PERGOLESI, from *LA SERVA PADRONA*
(The Maid Mistress)

1. Allegro

J.S. BACH, from *BAUERNKANTATE*
(Peasant Cantata)

2. Moderato

From 13th-century France

3.

Chorale Melody, *NUN DANKET ALLE GOTT*
(Now Thank We All Our God)

4.

JOHANNES BRAHMS, *SANDMÄNNCHEN*
(The Little Sandman)

V. ENSEMBLES

CARL PANDOLFI, Duet

MARC-ANTOINE CHARPENTIER, *MASS*

TONIC AND DOMINANT

Jules Massenet, from *Les Femmes de Magdala*

JULES MASSENET (1842–1912) was a French composer of opera at a time when Grand Opera, with its elaborate sets, complex plots, and nationalistic themes was all the rage in the Western world. Massenet entered the Paris Conservatory at the age of nine and later won prizes in piano and fugue. In 1863, at the age of twenty-one, he won the coveted *Prix de Rome,* granting him a lengthy stay in the Italian capital at state expense. Massenet, although a solidly romantic composer, wrote many operas that remain in the repertory today.

The melody below, from his composition *Les Femmes de Magdala,* illustrates the simplicity of traditional harmony. As you will learn, a *Triad* consists of three pitches spanning consecutive lines or spaces. Melodically the entire composition is comprised of the two most important triads in establishing a key: The *Tonic* and the *Dominant.* While composers typically employed many other chords for color, it is interesting to note that a sense of key can be established and maintained with a minimum of resources. This melody, in fact, is characteristic of many traditional compositions that, when reduced to their most basic elements, consist simply of progression from the tonic to the dominant, or the reverse.

JULES MASSENET, from *LES FEMMES DE MAGDALA*

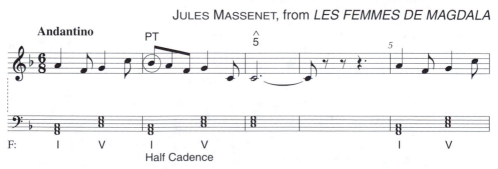

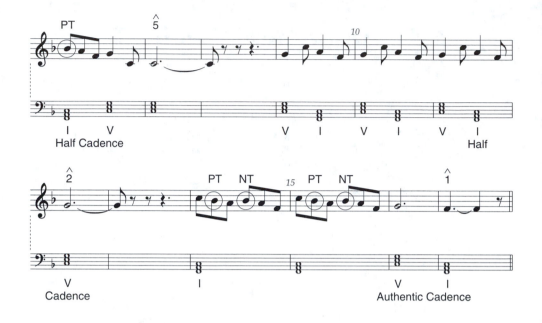

IN UNIT TWO

In Chapter 3 you will study root-position major triads as fundamental musical materials. You will also confront exercises and melodies featuring the tonic triad—the one built on the first scale degree. Further, in addition to simple meters already discussed, another type of metric scheme will be presented in which the beat divides into three parts, rather than two.

A series of triads designed to create the effect of tonality is known as a progression. One of the most important progressions in traditional music is the movement of the dominant triad to the tonic (or the reverse). Seen in several places in the melody from *Les Femmes de Magdala,* these progressions form cadences—points of harmonic and rhythmic emphasis used typically to conclude phrases. In Chapter 4 you will sing a variety of melodies and exercises involving both the tonic and dominant triads. You will further discover that while the beat in a compound meter divides into three parts, the beat *subdivides* into two parts just as it does in simple meters.

CHAPTER THREE

Intervals in the Tonic Triad
Compound Beat and Beat Division

Allied Theoretical Concepts
- Intervals
- Major Triads in Root Position and Inversion
- Diatonic Triads
- Passing and Neighboring Tones
- Compound Meter

Concepts in Pitch: Major Triads

A TRIAD is a group of three pitches. Since the end of the sixteenth century, much Western music has been based on a particular type of triad, termed TERTIAN, that is built of superimposed thirds.

Tertian Triads

ROOT-POSITION AND INVERTED TRIADS

When the root of a triad is also the BASS (lowest-sounding pitch), the triad is said to be in ROOT POSITION. A triad with the root above the bass is IN-VERTED. In FIRST INVERSION, the third is in the bass; the fifth is in the bass in SECOND INVERSION.

A major triad outline in root position is comprised of $\hat{1}$, $\hat{3}$, and $\hat{5}$. Stability in the root-position major triad results from the perfect fifth. Inverted, the major triad is comprised of the same scale degrees, but in an order that does not include the perfect fifth.

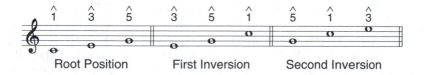

Root Position   First Inversion   Second Inversion

PASSING AND NEIGHBORING TONES

In the melody from Massenet's *Les Femmes de Magdala* (pages 29–30), you will notice several pitches circled on the score (measures 2, 6, 14, 15). These are NONHARMONIC TONES—pitches that appear in the melody, but lie outside the prevailing harmony. In *Les Femmes de Magdala*, most nonharmonic tones are PASSING TONES that merely fill in an interval of a third. Notice that passing tones may be either accented (m2, m6) or unaccented (m14-15).

NEIGHBORING TONES embellish a chord tone by step from above or below.

Passing Tones   Neighboring Tones

OCTAVE DESIGNATIONS

Each pitch name (A, B, F♯, and so on) appears in several different locations on the staff. OCTAVE DESIGNATION is a system for identifying a pitch in a particular octave. The method given here is one of several, but it is both the most simple and the one recommended by the American Society of Acoustics.

The pitch C is the lowest in each octave. "Middle" C is designated C_4; the octaves above and below respectively are C_5 and C_3.

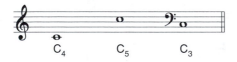

Pitches besides C are identified with the same octave designation number as the pitch C directly below them.

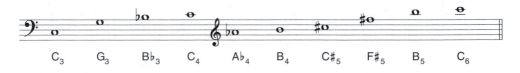

The three lowest notes on the standard piano keyboard are designated B_0, $B\flat_0$, and A_0 respectively. The highest pitch on the piano is C_8. The full range of pitches available on the standard keyboard is shown in the diagram opposite.

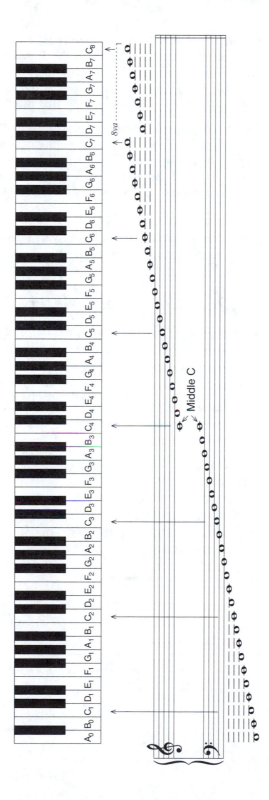

Range and Tessitura.   The construction of a melody may be studied through its RANGE (the interval between the highest and lowest pitches) and the TESSITURA—where *most* of the pitches lie (with higher and lower pitches excluded). In the Massenet melody, the range is narrow: from C_4 to C_5. The tessitura, however, would exclude the C_4 since this pitch is heard only four times.

Conjunct/Disjunct Motion.   Melodies that flow basically in step-wise motion are identified as CONJUNCT. Other melodies, based on triad outlines, move predominantly by leap and are classified as DISJUNCT. While most traditional melodies feature a balance between the two types of motion, refer to the passages listed below that are primarily conjunct and disjunct respectively.

Conjunct

Melodic Warm-up #8, page 37
Excerpt #3, page 41 (Strauss)

Disjunct

Melodic Warm-up #1, page 37
Excerpt #2, page 41 (Smetana)

Concepts in Rhythm: Compound Meter

You learned earlier about simple meters like $\frac{3}{4}$ in which the beat divides into two parts. An alternate metric system is COMPOUND METER. In a compound meter the beat is a dotted note that divides into three parts.

Simple Beat	Beat Division	Compound Beat	Beat Division

Counting Syllables in Compound Meters.   In a compound meter three syllables are necessary. The syllables "one-la-li" (pronounced "la-lee") are used for the beat divisions in compound meters. These alternate syllables differentiate clearly between simple and compound meters.

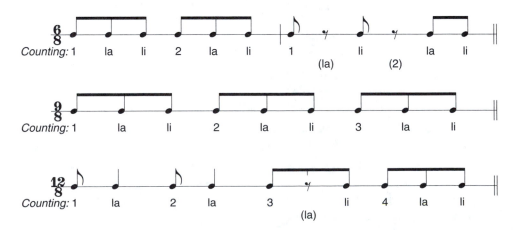

RHYTHMIC READING

I. WARM-UPS

Practice these basic patterns in compound meters as you did in the previous chapter: Sing them on a neutral syllable, perform them using counting syllables, and/or practice them as scales. In the last case, remember that each different beat should be performed on a different note of the scale.

Warm-up #5

Performed as Scale

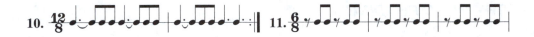

II. EXERCISES

Before you perform the rhythmic solos below, add tempo indications and specific performance instructions *in French*. Next, undertake an analysis of each solo considering motivic structure, cadences, repetition, and the like.

Composition.   Both of the solos above are eight measures in length. As directed, double the length of one or both of the solos to make sixteen-measure compositions. Several approaches to composing the second half of the solo are appropriate:

   a. Your second half might duplicate the first eight measures with only slight differences in material.
   b. Your second half might begin as the first did, but include some new material in the same style.
   c. You might use substantially contrasting material.
   d. Your second half could be a variation of the first.

In any event, maintain a consistent style in your composition and take care to make your calligraphy accurate and legible.

SIGHT SINGING

I. WARM-UPS

These simple exercises are comprised mainly of scales, gapped patterns and intervals within the tonic triad. Sing them using pitch names, solfège syllables, or a neutral syllable as directed.

II. EXERCISES

Analysis. Before performing the three melodies below, add tempo and performance instructions *in German*. Analyze each melody with regard to the following:

a. Where do outlines of the tonic triad appear? Are they in root position or inverted?

b. What is the balance between conjunct and disjunct motion?

c. What is the range? the tessitura? Be prepared to give both characteristics as intervals such as P5 and M10, or as exact pitch limits (B_3-$C\#_5$, Ab_4-G_5, and so on).

d. Consider the pitch inventory. Which pitch or pitches occur most frequently? Are any pitches in the scale absent? Where do melodic cadences occur?

e. Are passing or neighboring tones employed?

f. Can you identify principal melodic motives? Are there examples of sequence? What role (if any) does repetition play in the development of the melody?

III. STUDIES

Allegretto

2.

Poco allegro

3.

Piacevole

4.

Adagio

5.

IV. EXCERPTS FROM THE LITERATURE

HENRY III, *J'AI PERDU CELLE*
(I Have Lost Her)

SMETANA, from *THE BARTERED BRIDE*

JOHANN STRAUSS, *DIE FLEDERMAUS*
(The Bat)

English Folksong, *O CAN YE SEW CUSHIONS*

Allegro con moto

4.

Franz Schubert, *PAUSE*
(Rest)

Ziemlich geschwind

5.

V. ENSEMBLES

BENJAMIN BRITTEN, *HYMN TO ST. CECILIA*

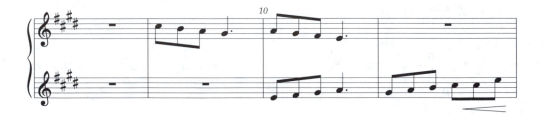

CHAPTER FOUR

Intervals in the Tonic and Dominant Triads

Compound Beat Subdivision

Allied Theoretical Concepts
- Major Triads in Root Position and Inversions
- Diatonic Triads
- Roman Numeral Analysis
- Authentic and Half Cadences
- Periodic Formal Structure

Concepts in Pitch: The Dominant Triad

The tonic triad represents tonal stability. The triad built on the fifth scale degree, however, the DOMINANT, is relatively unstable, since it contains the leading tone ($\hat{7}$). Notice that the dominant triad consists of $\hat{5}$, $\hat{7}$, and $\hat{2}$.

The movement of the dominant to the tonic, in fact, is one of the most important factors in establishing a feeling for key. Review the passage by Massenet, for example (page 29), and notice that the entire melody is based upon tonic and dominant triads. The roman numerals in the example indicate the root of the triad and its relationship to the tonic (I = tonic, V = dominant). The key, C major in this case, is shown with an uppercase letter followed by a colon.

Root-position and inverted dominant triads in major have intervals equivalent to those in the tonic triad: thirds and a perfect fifth (root position), or a perfect fourth plus a third and a sixth (inverted).

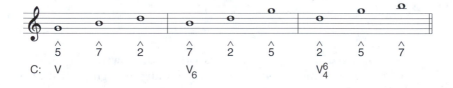

Tonal Tendencies

As long as a simple scale or a single triad is the basis of a melody (as in the preceding chapters), the tendency of one pitch to move to another is obvious. But when two different triads are involved (the tonic and dominant in this case), the strong tendency in one triad to move to a certain pitch in another triad is of significant value in sight singing. Other tendencies will be discussed in later chapters. For the present, however, $\hat{1}$, $\hat{3}$, and $\hat{5}$ in a major key are stable pitches. Moving from tonic to dominant, $\hat{2}$ has a relatively weak tendency to move to $\hat{1}$. The leading tone pitch, however ($\hat{7}$), tends to move to $\hat{8}$. These tendencies are especially strong following leaps.

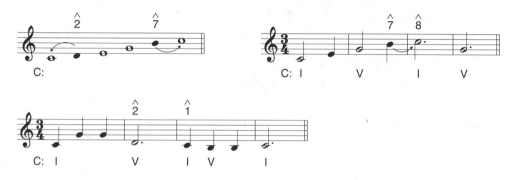

The Harmonic Half Cadence.   A CADENCE is a concluding formula used typically at the end of a phrase. When a phrase ends with the dominant triad, it is called a HALF CADENCE; the harmonic effect is relatively inconclusive (like a comma in sentence construction). The progression I–V is a common half cadence; the melodic cadence is progressive ($\hat{2}$, $\hat{5}$, or $\hat{7}$).

The Authentic Cadence.   When a progression of dominant to tonic ends a phrase, the cadence is known as AUTHENTIC and the harmonic effect is relatively conclusive (like a period). In a melodic context, the leading tone often ascends to the tonic.

Periodic Structure.   Two phrases, one ending with a half and the other with an authentic cadence, combine to form a larger formal unit known as a PERIOD. Taken together, the two phrases above constitute a period in form.

Since these two phrases begin with the same melodic material, they are classified as PARALLEL. Other periods have phrases that begin with different melodic ideas and are termed CONTRASTING. Study #2 on page 53 exemplifies contrasting periodic structure.

Melodic Analysis

You have already studied sequence—an important device used by composers to organize and unify a melody. When you understand the construction of a melody, the chances for an accurate performance—even at sight—are greatly increased.

Time-Line Analysis.   A TIME LINE is a graphic representation of form, key, cadences, motivic development, and other features as well. As shown below, time lines are usually divided in vertical lines to separate formal elements. Measure numbers and letters to identify phrases appear above the line; key identification and abbreviations to classify cadences appear below it. The time line shown below identifies the two phrases just discussed. Together, these two phrases constitute a parallel period.

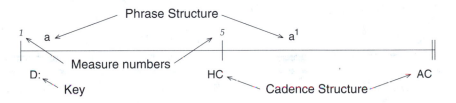

Step Progressions.   Well-constructed melodies often include STEP PROGRESSIONS—ascending or descending stepwise movement that usually occurs several beats apart. Normally, three pitches are required to constitute a step progression. In the two-phrase period below, step progressions are traced with horizontal lines. The implied harmonies are shown on the lower staff and analyzed with Roman numerals.

Vif

The Appoggiatura.   Passing and neighboring tones, discussed earlier, are types of nonharmonic tones. The APPOGGIATURA is another such figure that embellishes a chord tone from above or below, but is preceded by leap. The leap from a chord tone to a dissonance is followed by stepwise motion in the opposite direction to another chord tone. The structural reduction below is of the first two measures of Study 7 on page 54. An appoggiatura occurs on the second beat of the first measure. When you can identify the essential pitches of a melody and understand the ways those tones are embellished, sight singing will be greatly simplified.

Study 7

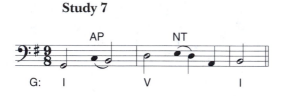

Concepts in Rhythm: The Compound Beat Subdivision

The subdivision of the beat in simple and compound meters is identical: The division subdivides into two parts. Where the beat in a compound meter divides into three parts, the subdivision is simple.

Counting Syllables.   Because the subdivision in simple and compound meters is identical, so are the syllables used in counting the rhythms. The syllable "ta" enunciates the subdivision.

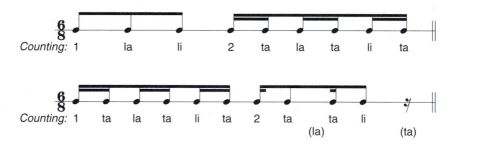

RHYTHMIC READING

I. WARM-UPS

Perform these brief exercises in a variety of ways as you have done in earlier chapters.

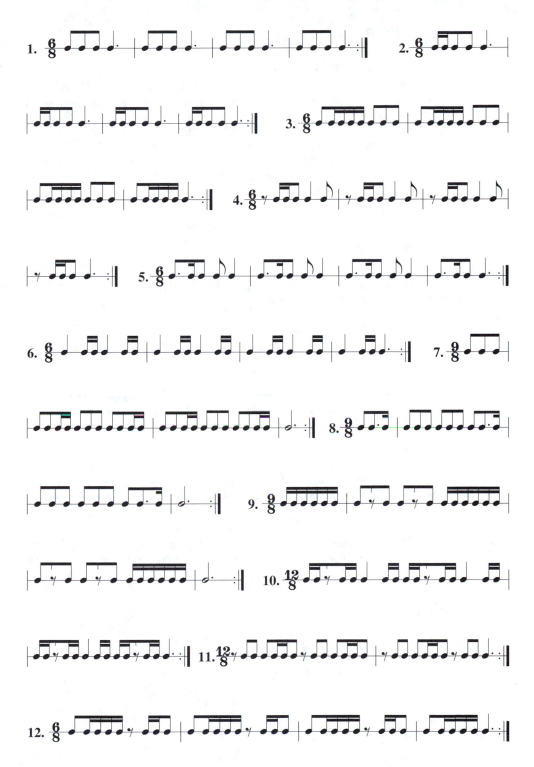

II. EXERCISES

Analysis.   Two rhythmic solos follow for performance and analysis. First, choose tempo and performance instructions *in Italian* that complement the rhythms. Next, analyze the solo in some or all of the following aspects:

a. What is the meter? the accent pattern?
b. How is the passage divided into phrases? A period? If so, how do phrases compare? Are they unified through repetition? Similar material? Contrasting material?
c. How varied are the rhythmic values employed? Do rests play a role in either of the solos?
d. Are there rhythmic motives present? If so, are they repeated? Varied? Use letters to identify motives and their variations (if any) on a time line.

After you have completed your analysis, perform the solos using counting syllables or another method.

SIGHT-SINGING

I. WARM-UPS

The brief passages that follow center on outlines of the tonic and dominant triads.

II. EXERCISES

Begin by choosing tempo and performance instructions *in French* that complement the music. Before performing the melodies, undertake a thorough analysis of both.

Composition.   Choose one of the melodies above and on a separate sheet, write at least one variation. Keep the harmony and cadential structure of the original intact, but embellish pitches, fill in between chord tones, and so on. You might also consider eliminating some of the pitches in the original to make a slower moving version. Perform the original melody followed by your variation(s).

III. STUDIES

Allegro

2.

Moderato

3.

Léger et gai

4.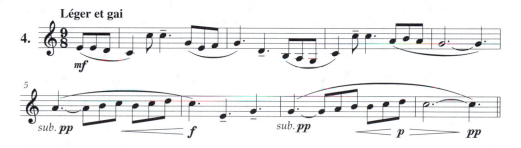

Leicht

5.

6. Marcato

7. Adagietto

8. Vite

Sehr ausdrucksvoll

9.

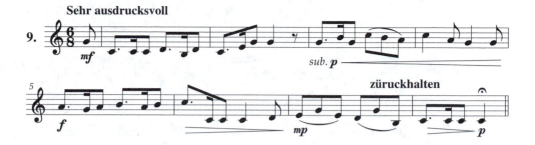

Deutlich

10.

IV. MELODIES FROM THE LITERATURE

FRANZ SCHUBERT, from *SYMPHONY NO. 5*

Allegro molto

1.

W. A. MOZART, from *DON GIOVANNI*

Allegro vivace

2.

W. A. Mozart, from *LE NOZZE DI FIGARO*
(The Marriage of Figaro)

Franz Schubert, *ANTONIUS UND CLEOPATRA*

V. ENSEMBLES

This second example is a CANON or ROUND in which the second voice (or group) enters at the beginning when the first voice reaches the point in the music marked "2."

HANS WACHSMANN, Canon for Two Voices

L. van Beethoven, SONATA, Op. 49, No. 2
(Simplified Arrangement)

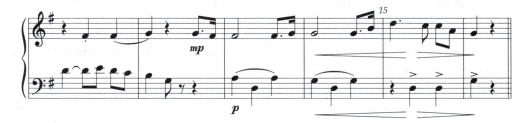

UNIT THREE

PRIMARY TONAL RESOURCES

Franz Schubert, *An der Frühling*

CHAPTER 5 The Primary Triads: Rests and Ties—Less Common Meters

CHAPTER 6 The Leading-Tone Triad and Dominant Seventh Chord: Syncopation

FRANZ SCHUBERT was born in 1797, a time when the Romantic movement was sweeping through Europe. Great German poets like Heine, Schiller, and Goethe provided texts about love, nature, and other humanist subjects that were set to music by composers like Schubert. These art songs, called *Lieder* (singular *lied*), were composed for trained singers and pianists. Yet while some truly innovative harmonies can be found in the nineteenth-century *lieder* literature, other works, like *An der Frühling* ("In Spring") are simple and straightforward in their construction.

FRANZ SCHUBERT, *AN DER FRÜHLING*

IN UNIT THREE

As you study the music of Schubert's *An der Frühling,* observe that the song is comprised of unpretentious harmonies based on triads (identified in Schubert's score with roman numerals below the staff). In addition to the tonic and dominant triads studied earlier, Chapter 5 introduces the subdominant, the triad built upon the fourth-scale degree. With the tonic and dominant, the subdominant completes the three functions employed in creating a tonal center. Embellished, filled in with stepwise movement, and occurring in various other arrangements, the primary triads form the basis of traditional harmony (measures 13–14 and 17–20). Many of the exercises and studies in this chapter center on rhythmic patterns that include rests, ties, and lesser notational values in simple and compound meters.

The concept of relative dissonance, discussed in Chapter 6, has intrigued composers and theorists since ancient times. Intervals like the *tritone* (augmented fourth and diminished fifth) and the major and minor seventh were resolved carefully and even forbidden altogether in certain circumstances.

But for composers like Schubert and his contemporaries, the subtle use of melodic and harmonic dissonance permitted a complex interplay of tension and stability. Just as $\hat{7}$ has an especially strong attraction to $\hat{8}$, the triad built on $\hat{7}$ is equally active. The leading tone triad (vii°) combines the momentum of $\hat{7}$ itself with the dissonant tritone between $\hat{4}$ and $\hat{7}$.

In addition to the leading tone triad, composers create even stronger sensations of momentum by adding a seventh above the root of a simple triad to form a seventh chord. The dominant seventh chord (a major triad with minor seventh above the root) is by far the most common harmonic dissonance used by Common Practice composers.

Since metric rhythm became common sometime after 1200, composers have used various techniques to enliven a given meter. Syncopation—the intentional misplacement of accents, is one of these devices. Many of the exercises and studies in Chapter 6 feature syncopated patterns as well as notation in half-note and dotted half-note meters.

CHAPTER FIVE

The Primary Triads
Rests and Ties—Less Common Meters

Allied Theoretical Concepts
- The Subdominant
- Function

Concepts in Pitch: Function in Melody

The establishment of a tonal center was of paramount importance to Common Practice composers. Accordingly, traditional compositions are typically based on the three PRIMARY TRIADS—those with roots on the tonic, dominant, and subdominant pitches respectively. These are the triads with the strongest ability to define a key. While the tonic and dominant triads alone can establish a tonal center, when the subdominant (IV) is added to a progression, the feeling for key is enhanced.

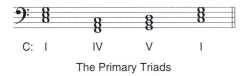

C: I   IV   V   I

The Primary Triads

The subdominant triad is major in quality and includes $\hat{4}$, $\hat{6}$, and $\hat{1}$.

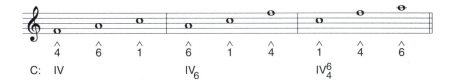

$\hat{4}$ $\hat{6}$ $\hat{1}$ $\hat{6}$ $\hat{1}$ $\hat{4}$ $\hat{1}$ $\hat{4}$ $\hat{6}$

C: IV   IV$_6$ IV$_4^6$

Function.   FUNCTION is a term describing the the role of an individual triad or pitch in creating a sense of tonality in the mind of the listener. The tonic, subdominant, and dominant triads represent three different functions. Juxtaposed between the stability of the tonic triad and the momentum of the dominant, the subdominant represents a midpoint or *predominant* position in a tonal progression.

In a melodic sense, $\hat{1}$ and $\hat{3}$ represent a tonic (stable) function; $\hat{4}$ and $\hat{6}$ are typically predominant, and $\hat{2}$, $\hat{5}$, and especially $\hat{7}$ have dominant function. These tendencies are especially pronounced following a leap, or with pitches appearing in strong metric positions.

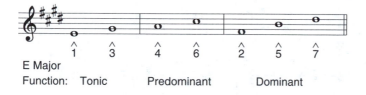

E Major
Function: Tonic   Predominant   Dominant

The Anticipation. Another common nonharmonic tone, the ANTICIPATION, precedes ("anticipates") the same tone in the next chord that is consonant. As shown below, a dotted rhythm is often associated with the anticipation.

HARMONIC REDUCTION

The ability to "reduce" a melody to its essential structural framework can be a great aid in sight singing. Observe the first two phrases of *An der Frühling* and their reduction. STRUCTURAL PITCHES, the most important chord tones, are shown as half notes; SECONDARY PITCHES, or less important chord tones (principally those on weak beats and/or with lesser rhythmic values), appear as quarter notes. EMBELLISHING PITCHES, like neighboring tones, are represented with stemless noteheads and the appropriate abbreviation. Finally, passing tones (which merely fill in between chord tones and therefore have no harmonic role) are omitted from a reduction.

- ♩ = Structural Pitches

- ♩ = Secondary Pitches

- • = Embellishing Pitches

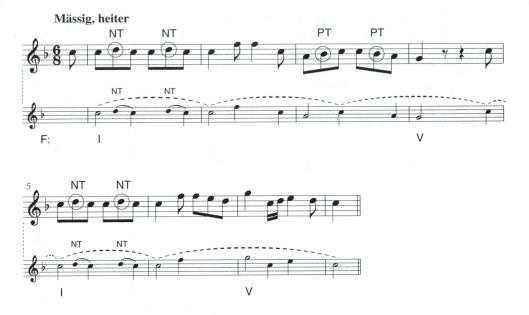

Prolongation. A single pitch sometimes plays a structural role over a period of several beats or several measures. Such emphasis on one pitch is called a PROLONGATION and is indicated on the reduction above with dashed lines. Prolongation can be thought of as the influence exerted by a note over a span of time, even though that note may not be present physically at every instant.

Reduction

You will notice that, when reduced, the structural pitches of the melody above outline a tonic triad. This structure is typical of traditional melodic construction.

Concepts in Rhythm: Rests and Ties

Composers use rests and ties both to vary the natural accents of a given meter and to create certain effects that are appropriate to the nature of the composition. As in the following example, passages that combine ties and rests can appear intimidating.

Gehend

The use of counting syllables will help in sight reading. When practice is possible, begin by eliminating the ties and adding in pitches in place of the rests. When you can perform the simplified version, gradually replace the pitches with rests and reinstate the ties.

1   (2) te   3   te   (1) ta te   2 ta (te) ta 3   (1) ta te ta 2   te   (1)

LESS COMMON METERS

While composers often employ meters such as $\frac{2}{4}$ and $\frac{6}{8}$, other meter signatures are common as well. If an eighth-note beat is desired for a simple meter, a composer might use $\frac{2}{8}$ or $\frac{3}{8}$ for the meter signature. Likewise, a dotted half-note beat could be reflected in meters like $\frac{6}{4}$ and $\frac{9}{4}$. Beat division and subdivision are notated exactly as they are in quarter- and dotted quarter-note meters.

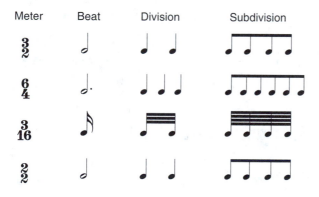

Meter	Beat	Division	Subdivision

RHYTHMIC READING

I. WARM-UPS

II. EXERCISES

As in previous chapters, select tempo, dynamic, and expression indications for both of the exercises below. Use terms *in English* as well as conventional Italian dynamic signs.

Composition.   TRANSCRIPTION is the process of changing the notation of music so that, while the new version differs from the original in appearance, a performance will *sound* exactly the same. Given an original meter like $\frac{3}{4}$, for example, transcriptions might be made in $\frac{3}{8}$ or $\frac{3}{2}$.

Original

Transcriptions

Likewise, compositions originally in $\frac{6}{8}$ might be transcribed into $\frac{6}{4}$, $\frac{6}{2}$, $\frac{6}{16}$, or any duple-compound meter.

Original

Transcriptions

Transcribe the two rhythmic solos above as follows:
a. Transcribe the first solo from $\frac{2}{4}$ to $\frac{2}{2}$ (¢).
b. Transcribe the second solo from $\frac{6}{8}$ to $\frac{6}{4}$.

SIGHT SINGING

I. WARM-UPS

As directed, transcribe one or more of these warm-ups to a different meter.

II. EXERCISES

Analysis. For the two melodies below, add tempo and other specific performance instructions *in German*. Before performance, follow the guidelines on page 38 and analyze both melodies.

Composition.   On a separate sheet, and as directed, write two different variations of one or both of the melodies shown above. Maintain the same harmony, but consider varying rhythm, melody, or meter. Variations of the first melody, for example, might begin as shown below.

Variation I

Variation II

III. STUDIES

Andante

4.

mf cantabile

più mosso

a tempo

mp

Valse

5.

f

1.

2.

Andante timoroso

6.

mp

p

poco stringendo

tempo primo

p

p

mf

mp

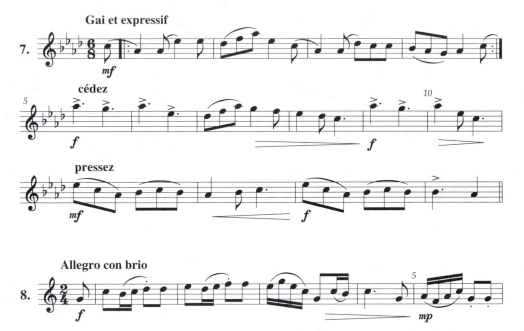

Modéré

10.

IV. EXCERPTS FROM THE LITERATURE

HUGO WOLF, *THE GARDNER*

Leicht, graziös

1.

L. VAN BEETHOVEN, *DAS BLÜMCHEN WUNDERHOLD*
(Exquisite Little Flowers)

Andante

2.

CARL MARIA VON WEBER, Variations

L. VAN BEETHOVEN, *MIT EINEM GEMALTEN BAND*
(With a Painted Ribbon)

L. VAN BEETHOVEN, Sonata in G Major

CHRISTOPH GLUCK, from *ORPHEUS*

V. ENSEMBLES

GIACOMO PUCCINI, from *MESSA DI GLORIA*

Allegro ma non troppo

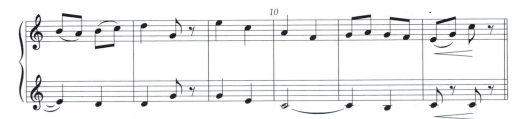

IGNAZ JOSEPH PLEYEL, Duet

Tempo di Minuetto

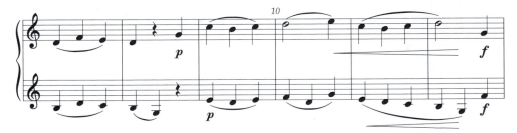

The Leading-Tone Triad and Dominant Seventh Chord
Syncopation

Allied Theoretical Concepts
- Seventh Chords in Root Position and Inversions
- The Tritone
- Consonance and Dissonance
- Syncopation

Concepts in Pitch: Harmonic Dissonance

Intervals like perfect fifths and perfect octaves have been discussed in this text as being relatively stable. CONSONANCE is a term often applied to stable intervals. Relatively unstable intervals, on the other hand, are DISSONANT; the more dissonant an interval sounds, the stronger its tendency will be to resolve to a consonance. The TRITONE (augmented fourth or diminished fifth) is the single most dissonant interval in traditional music. Harmonically, the augmented fourth resolves typically to a consonant major or minor sixth; the diminished fifth usually progresses to a major or minor third.

G: A4   m6   d5   M3

The Leading-Tone Triad.   The triad built on $\hat{7}$ of a major scale is termed the LEADING-TONE TRIAD and is diminished in quality (with minor third and diminished fifth above the root). Where the perfect fifth in major triads provides stability, the tritone between the root and the fifth of the leading-tone triad is inherently unstable. In analysis, a diminished triad is indicated by a small circle which emphasizes its unstable nature (vii°).

A♭:   vii°   vii°₆

In a melodic context, $\hat{7}$ usually progresses to $\hat{8}$; $\hat{4}$ characteristically descends to $\hat{3}$.

In measures 19–20 of *An der Frühling* (page 000), a melodic tritone appears in conjunction with the final authentic cadence ($\hat{7}$ then resolves to $\hat{8}$).

The Dominant Seventh Chord

When a seventh is added above the root of a triad, the resulting sonority is known as a SEVENTH CHORD. A seventh chord is a HARMONIC DISSONANCE as opposed to a melodic dissonance such as a passing tone. In analysis, an arabic numeral 7 is added to the roman numeral symbol to designate a root-position seventh chord. The numerals $^6_5$, $^4_3$, and $^4_2$ respectively, designate inverted sevenths. The dominant seventh (V^7) consists of a major triad with a minor seventh above the root and is therefore also known as a "major-minor" seventh chord.

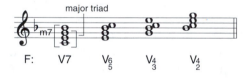

In melodies, seventh chords are outlined just as triads are (although all four pitches are rarely heard in succession). Almost invariably, the dissonant seventh of a dominant seventh chord ($\hat{4}$) resolves down by step to $\hat{3}$. This is true whether the dissonant interval is a seventh (root position) or a second (inverted).

In the final two measures of *An der Frühling,* the tritone Bb-E is part of a dominant seventh chord (C-E-G-Bb). As mentioned previously, the pitch E resolves to F. Had the interval ascended (E-Bb), however, the Bb (the seventh of the chord) would probably have resolved down to A ($\hat{4}$-$\hat{3}$).

Concepts in Rhythm: Syncopation

When composers choose a meter (an accent pattern and either the simple or the compound beat division), they normally retain that plan until the listener has time to perceive it as "normal." As discussed earlier, this is called METRIC ACCENT. Three other types of accent exist in traditional music.

- DYNAMIC ACCENT results from a pitch that is louder than others surrounding it. Dynamic accent is indicated with the symbol >.
- AGOGIC ACCENT occurs when a pitch is relatively longer than others.
- TONIC (or TONAL ACCENT) is created when one note is relatively higher or lower than those adjacent to it.

Dynamic Accents   Agogic Accent   Tonic Accent

Within a given metric framework, a composer typically creates variety through one or more standard techniques. One of the most important of these centers on accent and is termed SYNCOPATION.

Syncopation is the intentional misplacement of accents. In the passage below, the agogic accent on the second beat (measures 2–3) creates a moderate feeling of displacement.

When syncopation occurs at the level of the beat division, the effect is more pronounced. The passage below includes syncopation figures involving the beat division (measures 2 and 4) as well as the subdivision (measure 7).

Learning Syncopated Melodies. If a syncopated passage is difficult for you, rewrite the line using as a common denominator the smallest rhythmic value in the pattern. Renotate the passage using ties in place of longer values. Practice the melody without the ties and with notes of the appropriate values substituted for rests; when you can perform the renotated version, reinstate the ties and rests.

Original

Renotated for Practice

The Breve.   In half-note and dotted half-note meters you will occasionally encounter the BREVE—an older rhythmic symbol twice the value of the whole note. Observe in the example below that the breve rest fills the entire third space on the staff.

Breve   Rest

RHYTHMIC READING

I. WARM-UPS

Due to the displacement of beats in syncopated patterns, you should practice the warm-ups below on *a single pitch* rather than with a scale as you have done previously.

II. EXERCISES

Analysis.   Add tempo and performance instructions *in Italian* to the two rhythmic solos below. Analyze the passages for rhythmic and metric content, motivic usage, and variety, as usual (see page 50). In the study of these passages, also consider the following:

    a. To what extent (if any) does syncopation occur? If present, is syncopation at the beat, division, or subdivision level?

    b. In terms of rhythmic content alone, what is the form of the solo? Is it a phrase? a period? How would you label the phrase structure (a, b, a^1, and so on)?

After you have concluded your analyses, perform the solos with counting syllables.

SIGHT SINGING

I. WARM-UPS

II. EXERCISES

Add tempo and performance instructions *in French* to the two melodies below. Prior to performance, study the passages in terms of their melodic content (see page 38 for a list of possible topics).

Composition.   Choose one or both of the periodic melodies above, and on a separate sheet, extend it with two additional phrases to form a double period. Use appropriate cadences for the third and fourth phrases and provide structural analysis and/or a timeline graph as directed. Consider three possible approaches to the composition of the second period:

a. Use a different motive for the material of the third phrase and return to the original music for the fourth.
b. Begin the third phrase with a variation of the original material; develop a contrasting motive for the fourth and final phrase.
c. Duplicate the first and second phrases, but vary them substantially.

III. STUDIES

Langsam

3.

Andante sostenuto

4.

Allegro giocoso

5.

Immer geshwind

6.

Mässig und feierlich

7.

etwas schnell

Einfach, nicht langsam

8.

Moderato

9.

IV. EXCERPTS FROM THE LITERATURE

W. A. MOZART, *DIE IHR UNERMESSLICHEN WELTALLS*
(Ye Who the World's Creator)

W. A. Mozart, *DIE KLEINE SPINNERIN*
(The Little Spinner)

W. A. Mozart, from *DON GIOVANNI*

Franz Schubert, *DAS WANDERN*
(The Wanderer)

JOHANNES SCHOLZ, *ICH BIN NUN WIE ICH BIN*
(I am only as I am)

FELIX MENDELSSOHN, Concerto in D Minor

PHILIPPE VERDELOT, *ONE SMILING SUMMER MORNING*

V. ENSEMBLES

CLAUDIO MONTEVERDI, from *THE CORONATION OF POPPEA*

James Greeson, Duet

A. J. Morrison, *DELIBERATE DISTURBANCE*

UNIT FOUR

THE MINOR MODE

Henry Purcell, "Ye Twice Ten Hundred Deities" from *The Indian Queen*

HENRY PURCELL (1659–95) is one of the greatest of English composers. In his short life he wrote sonatas and other instrumental works, arias, keyboard compositions, an opera (*Dido and Aeneas*), and a tremendous amount of "incidental" music to accompany the performance of stage plays. "Ye Twice Ten Hundred Deities" is an aria from music Purcell wrote for the play *The Indian Queen* (1695), by Dryden and Howard.

The melody of "Ye Twice Ten Hundred Deities" (page 96) is simple, yet it illustrates the use of the minor mode and various chromatic alterations that are associated with it. The work is in G minor and the key signature of two flats is not exceptional. Yet the presence of F♯ in measures 4, 10, 12, and 14, plus the E-natural in measure 12, require explanation.

The minor mode is the subject of Unit 4. For the present, notice that while the pitch F would be natural in G minor, Purcell used F♯ to provide a leading tone, as would be found in G major. Likewise, where we would expect an E♭, E-natural appears in measure 12. Unlike diatonic pitches in major, certain variations are common in minor.

In addition to the chromatic alterations seen in "Ye Twice Ten Hundred Deities," notice the undulating melodic curve and limited range (a minor seventh), the simplicity of rhythmic values, the primary harmony, and the regular periodic structure.

HENRY PURCELL, "Ye Twice Ten Hundred Deities,"
from *THE INDIAN QUEEN*

IN UNIT FOUR

Prior to about 1550, composers based their music on a variety of scale patterns called *modes*. The major scale was known then as IONIAN MODE. While all modes were theoretically available to Common Practice composers, they limited themselves almost exclusively to just two of them: Major and Minor. You have already studied the major scale and the primary triads in major keys. The present unit will center on these same materials in minor.

In Chapter 7, you will learn to sing three different forms of the minor scale known as natural, harmonic, and melodic respectively. Although we commonly study these scales as if they were three distinct choices, you will find that composers choose melodic patterns in minor that emphasize the goal of the passage. The emphasis in Chapter 7 is on singing the scales themselves (along with gapped patterns including thirds and fifths).

A sense of key is established through strong progressions in minor just as it is in major. As you work through Chapter 8, you will find that the minor melodies like Purcell's "Ye Twice Ten Hundred Deities" consist of scale patterns together with outlines of the tonic and dominant triads.

While simple and compound meters were discussed earlier as virtually opposite choices, Chapter 8 introduces borrowed division—an alternate rhythmic possibility with a three-part division in a simple meter.

The melodies in Chapter 9 involve the primary triads in minor as well as various forms of the minor scale itself. In terms of rhythm and meter, the borrowed (two-part) division in compound meters is highlighted.

CHAPTER SEVEN

The Minor Scale
Emphasis on Dotted Rhythms

Allied Theoretical Concepts
- Natural, Harmonic, and Melodic Minor Scales
- The Leading Tone and Subtonic
- The Major and Minor "Effects"

Concepts in Pitch: Minor Scales

What we now call the minor scale was known originally as AEOLIAN MODE. The whole- and half-step pattern of this series is W H W W H W W. Today we call this scale NATURAL or PURE MINOR. Compare the A-major and A-natural minor scales shown below.

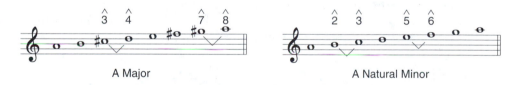

A Major   A Natural Minor

Leading Tone and Subtonic. Like the major scale, the natural minor scale is comprised of five whole and two half steps. Notice in the previous example that in major, the half steps fall between $\hat{3}$ and $\hat{4}$ and between $\hat{7}$ and $\hat{8}$. In natural minor, there are half steps between $\hat{2}$ and $\hat{3}$ and between $\hat{5}$ and $\hat{6}$.

As discussed earlier, $\hat{7}$ in major is a leading tone and, by definition, lies a diatonic half step below the tonic. In natural minor, however, $\hat{7}$ is a *whole* step below the tonic; this seventh degree is termed a SUBTONIC.

Harmonic Minor. Because the pull of the leading tone to tonic aided composers in establishing a feeling for key, they often raised the subtonic to provide a leading tone in minor. This practice is especially common in harmony (as opposed to melody) and is known as HARMONIC MINOR. Compared with natural minor, harmonic minor has a raised $\hat{7}$; compared to major, $\hat{3}$ and $\hat{6}$ are lowered.

E Natural Minor   E Harmonic Minor   E Major

Melodic Minor.   When composers raised $\hat{7}$ in minor melodies, an awkward interval called an AUGMENTED SECOND (consisting of three half steps) was formed between $\hat{6}$ and raised $\hat{7}$. To avoid this problem, $\hat{6}$ was often raised as well. This new form of minor is known as MELODIC.

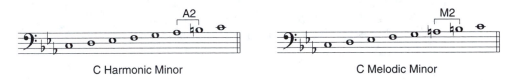

C Harmonic Minor   C Melodic Minor

If a melodic pattern descends, raised $\hat{7}$ is not normally used; raised $\hat{6}$ is thus unnecessary as well. The descending form of melodic minor has a natural $\hat{6}$ and $\hat{7}$—the same as natural minor.

Ascending and Descending Melodic Minor

The use of raised $\hat{6}$ or $\hat{7}$ in minor makes many melodic patterns equivalent to those you have already learned in major. Comparing the first five pitches of major with the three forms of minor, only $\hat{3}$ is different. This is the MODAL DEGREE that establishes the major or minor effect.

Major   Natural, Harmonic, and Melodic Minor

Within the upper four pitches (termed a *tetrachord*) major and ascending melodic minor are identical; harmonic and natural minors differ from major only in $\hat{6}$ and $\hat{7}$.

Major/ Melodic Minor   Harmonic Minor   Natural Minor

Melodic Attractions in Minor.   As in major, $\hat{1}$, $\hat{3}$, and $\hat{5}$ in minor are stable pitches to which others in the scale gravitate. The strongest tendencies are the same as in major: $\hat{7}$-$\hat{8}$ and $\hat{4}$-$\hat{3}$. Also as in major, melodic attractions are strongest following a leap. In the passage below, the movement of $\hat{7}$-$\hat{8}$ stresses the key center; the *mode* is emphasized as $\hat{4}$ moves to $\hat{3}$.

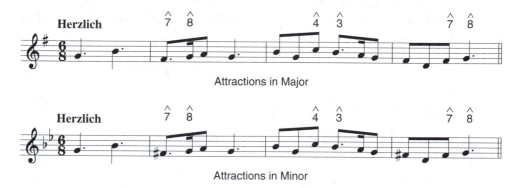

Attractions in Major

Attractions in Minor

Melodies move typically according to the *goal* of a given passage, as shown below. If the tonic is the goal of an ascending passage, raised $\hat{6}$ and/or $\hat{7}$ will be employed. If the dominant is the goal, however, either or both of these same pitches will probably be natural.

Tonic as Goal

Dominant as Goal

When pitches other than the tonic and dominant are emphasized, raised or lowered $\hat{6}$ and/or $\hat{7}$ reflect the direction of the passage. The Renaissance melody "La Folia" (the Fool) below, for example, illustrates the characteristic use of raised $\hat{7}$ to emphasize the tonic. In measure 3, however, the goal is not D, but E and the subtonic is used.

As in the case of most all accidentals in tonal music, when you analyze a passage and discern the relative importance of individual pitches, music that initially seemed difficult often seems much easier. Use melodic reduction to isolate the structural pitches, then study the roles of other pitches as they relate to short-term melodic goals.

Concepts in Rhythm: Multiple Dotting

The dotted-eighth and sixteenth patterns in both simple and compound meters were introduced earlier. This chapter includes a review of these and other dotted-note idioms. In addition to values with a single dot, however, two and even three dots sometimes follow a note or rest. The principle of dotted notes applies regardless of the number of dots: Each dot receives one half the value preceding it.

CÉSAR FRANCK, Quintet for Piano and Strings

In the rare instances where composers use three or more dots, the notation usually means simply "make the following note as short as possible."

RHYTHMIC READING

I. WARM-UPS

The warm-ups in this and following chapters should be sung using major as well as all three forms of minor scales. Change pitches on each beat as you did in earlier chapters.

II. EXERCISES

Add tempo and performance instructions *in Italian* to the following rhythmic solos. Next, undertake a thorough analysis of one or both of them.

Composition.   Choose one of the solos above, and on a separate sheet, write a series of three rhythmic variations in addition to the original. The variations may be the same length and form, or they may be different. Be certain that you make the original motives apparent in the variations, however. Consider the following structure:

Variation I   Change the meter, but use similar motives to the original (𝄴 ♩ ♩ ♩ might become 𝄵 ♩. ♩ ♩ ♩ ♪, for example).

Variation II   Return to the original meter, but change the tempo, dynamics, and at least one aspect of the original rhythms.

Variation III   Add notes to the original solo so that the movement is generally in smaller note values than the original.

Be careful with your calligraphy and make performance instructions explicit and detailed.

SIGHT-SINGING

I. WARM-UPS

These brief exercises consist of scale and gapped-scale patterns. While harmonic implications exist ($\hat{1}$ to $\hat{5}$, for example, as i–V, or $\hat{5}$ to $\hat{1}$ as V–i), think of the pitches in these exercises as degrees within the minor scale. The first three warm-ups are complete scales and should be sung on a variety of pitches throughout your range.

The next three warm-ups are in major, but are followed by similar versions in minor. First sing the major melody and feel the stability of $\hat{1}$, $\hat{3}$, and $\hat{5}$. Next, sing the minor version and notice that these same three scale degrees are points of stability in the minor mode. The first and fifth scale degrees, in fact, are identical in major and minor.

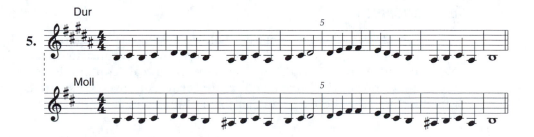

These warm-ups include gapped-scale patterns in minor.

II. EXERCISES

Analysis.   The two melodies below are stepwise and gapped-scale patterns in minor. Begin by adding tempo and performance instructions *in French*. Next, analyze each melody thoroughly in terms of scale content. Is one form of minor used throughout? Are two or more forms employed? If so, speculate on why the composer chose a particular form of minor in each given situation.

1.

5

2.

III. STUDIES

Allegro guisto

1.

Moderato

2.

più mosso

Allegro agitato

3.

Allegro spiritoso

4.

5

Fliessand

5.

10

zurückhalten

Marziale

6.

IV. EXCERPTS FROM THE LITERATURE

W. A. Mozart, *MASS*, K. 427

Konrad Künz, Canon

THÉODORE DUBOIS, from *THE LAST SEVEN WORDS*

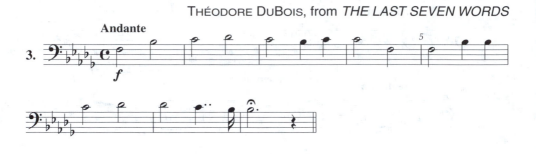

LEOPOLD MOZART, *BOURREÉ*

L. VAN BEETHOVEN, *MARMOTTE*

Renaissance Melody, *LA FOLIA*
("The Fool")

V. ENSEMBLES

French Folk Song
(Lower voice by Robert Ottman)

2.

Fröhlich

FINE AND YOUNG GREEN WATERCRESS
(Traditional English Round)

3.

Larghetto

CHAPTER EIGHT

The Tonic, Dominant, and Dominant-Seventh Chords in Minor
Borrowed Division in Simple Meters

Allied Theoretical Concepts
- Diatonic Triads in Minor
- The Natural and Borrowed Divisions of the Beat

Concepts in Pitch: The Tonic and Dominant Triads in Minor

In minor keys, the tonic triad is minor in quality. A root-position minor triad has a minor third and a perfect fifth above its root. The upper third is major.

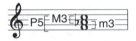

Melodically, the minor triad in root position and inversions duplicates the intervals found in the major triad: major and minor thirds and sixths as well as perfect fifth and perfect fourth.

| Root Position | First Inversion | Second Inversion |

The Dominant. While $\hat{7}$ in a major scale is a leading tone (a half step below the tonic), $\hat{7}$ in minor is a subtonic—a pitch lying a whole step below the tonic. The seventh scale degree is the third of the dominant triad. In major keys, the dominant triad is major in quality; without alteration, the same triad in minor keys is minor.

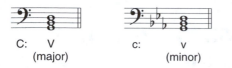

C: V   c: v
(major)   (minor)

Composers liked the sound of the leading tone in major, however, and utilized its strong effect in establishing a sense of tonality in minor keys as well. Traditional composers simply raised $\hat{7}$ a half step to produce the leading tone. The raised $\hat{7}$ appears as the third in the dominant triad making the quality major, rather than minor. While a minor key signature always reflects *natural* minor, the raised $\hat{7}$ appears as an accidental.

c: v   V
    Minor Triad   Major Triad
    (Very Rare)   (Common)

In many melodies the raised $\hat{6}$ and $\hat{7}$ are used as discussed in Chapter 7, but when the dominant triad is outlined in a melody, the raised $\hat{7}$ is nearly always employed. As a result, passages like that below, in which both the natural and the raised $\hat{7}$ appear, are common in traditional music.

Moderato, poco andante

The Dominant Seventh Chord in Minor.   The term "dominant seventh" specifies a chord that consists of a major triad with a minor seventh above the root. Accordingly, both the dominant triad and the dominant seventh chord are the same in major and minor. In minor, an accidental is necessary to make the triad major.

D: V   V⁷   d: V   V⁷   E♭: V   V⁷   e♭: V   V⁷

Concepts in Rhythm: Borrowed Division

As you have learned, the beat in simple meters divides into two parts. This is called the NATURAL BEAT DIVISION. While a composer must choose either a simple or compound beat division for the basic metric structure of a composition, the alternate possibility—the BORROWED DIVISION—is always available for use on a temporary basis. In a simple meter, the borrowed division is the TRIPLET, which divides the beat into three, rather than two parts. The numeral 3 always accompanies a triplet figure to indicate that the notes are to be performed faster than those of the natural division.

Counting The Borrowed Division.   Where the syllable "te" is used for the beat division in a simple meter, "la" and "li" facilitate the performance of a triplet just as they do with the natural compound beat division. The familiar three-part syllable division is *borrowed* from compound meter for temporary use in a simple meter.

Likewise when three notes are grouped together as a triplet, they are to be performed on a single beat.

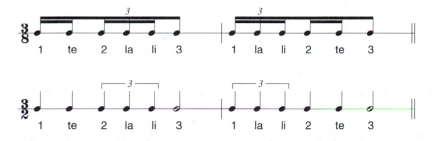

Borrowed division in compound meters and variations of the borrowed division will be covered in later chapters.

RHYTHMIC READING

I. SCALE WARM-UPS

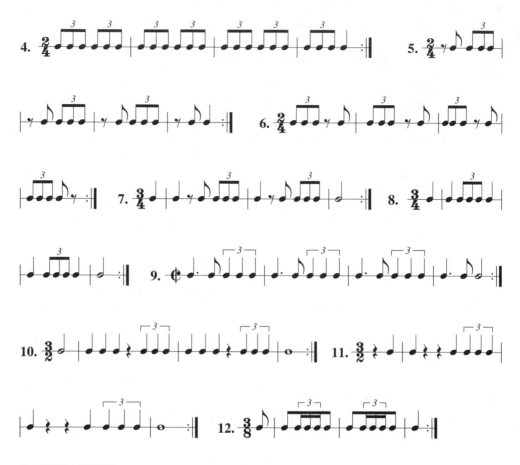

II. EXERCISES

Choose tempo and performance instructions *in French* and add them to the solos below. Before performance, analyze the rhythmic content in detail. In addition to areas of analysis already discussed, locate and be prepared to comment on instances of borrowed division.

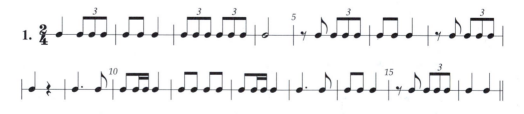

2. $\frac{3}{8}$

Composition. Choose one or both of the solos above and write a second part below the one given. The second part should employ motives that are clearly related to the first, but it should be subordinate, generally moving in slower and less distinctive rhythms. Be aware that if you employ the natural and borrowed divisions of the beat simultaneously (as shown below), you will create the effect of "two against three," which some performers find difficult. Include performance instructions for the second part that complement those of the solo.

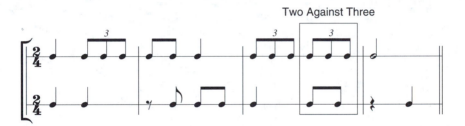

Two Against Three

SIGHT-SINGING

I. WARM-UPS

As in Chapter 7, the first three warm-ups in minor are preceded by versions in major. Compare the two melodies and study the melodic attractions in both modes. With the exception of $\hat{3}$ (the modal degree), you will find that major and minor are quite similar. The techniques you used in singing melodies based on tonic and dominant triads in major are applicable in minor as well.

1. **Maggiore**

Minore

Dur

2.

Moll

Majeur

3.

Mineur

4.

5.

6.

7.

5

8.

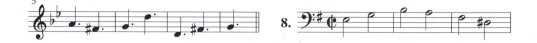

II. EXERCISES

Add performance and tempo indications *in German* to the two melodies below. Before performance, conduct an analysis as discussed in previous chapters.

Composition. Choose one or both of the previous melodies and write two variations. Make your variations approximately the same length, form, style, and level-of-performance difficulty as the original. Use only those musical materials that have been covered to this point in the text. If you use melodic patterns that imply a dominant seventh chord, be sure to resolve the seventh down by step. This may not be necessary, however, if another member of the seventh chord *follows* the seventh. Add tempo and performance instructions in English.

Consider choices for variation such as these:

a. Retain the harmony, but choose different pitches within the original chords. Use generally slower-moving rhythms.

b. Embellish pitches of the original melody with nonharmonic tones.

c. Change the meter of the original melody so that a new version emerges within the same harmonic and melodic framework.

d. Change the key signature to that of the relative major and adjust any accidentals in the original as necessary. (Of course you will ignore in the major version raised $\hat{6}$ and/or $\hat{7}$.) Variations in major of a melody originally in minor are often labeled "Maggiore."

III. STUDIES

Allegro spirito

1.

Energico

2.

Tempo di valse

3.
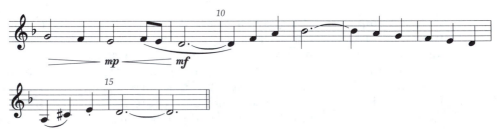

Modéré

4.

5. **Etwas kräftig**

6. **Adagietto**

7. **Gehend**

8.

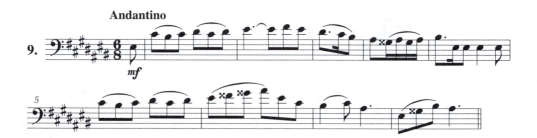

D.C. al Fine

9.

10.

IV. EXCERPTS FROM THE LITERATURE

P. I. TCHAIKOVSKY, *DON JUAN'S SERENADE*

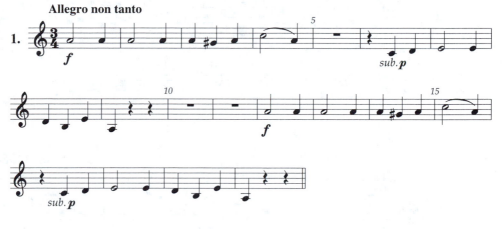

W. A. MOZART, Quartet in D Minor, K. 421

L. VAN BEETHOVEN, Sonata in E Minor

W. A. Mozart, *ICH WÜRD AUF MEINEM PFAD*
(The Pathway that I Tread)

L. van Beethoven, *AIR COSAQUE*

Franz Schubert, *ERSTARRUNG*
(Numbness)

V. ENSEMBLES

1.

JOSEPH HAYDN, *CANON FOR THREE VOICES*

2.

CHAPTER NINE

The Primary Triads in Minor
Borrowed Division in Compound Meters

Allied Theoretical Concepts
- ■ Diatonic Triads in Minor
- ■ The Natural and Borrowed Divisions of the Beat
- ■ Equivalent Meters

Concepts in Pitch: The Primary Triads in Minor

The tonic triad is typically minor in quality. Likewise, as you have learned, the dominant triad in minor keys is almost invariably major (with raised $\hat{7}$ as the third). The subdominant triad (with $\hat{6}$ as the third) is most often minor, although the major subdominant, with raised $\hat{6}$, is not uncommon.

d: i   V   iv   or   IV

In a melodic setting, either of the passages below is possible.

Picardy Third. A common alteration of the tonic triad in minor is the PICARDY THIRD—a raised $\hat{3}$ in the tonic triad of a final cadence. The Picardy third is especially prevalent in the Baroque Era (ca. 1600–1750).

Picardy
Third

Concepts in Rhythm: Borrowed Division in Compound Meters

In the last chapter, you learned that a triplet allows a three-part division of a simple beat. The DUPLET allows the compound (three-part) beat to be divided into two parts. The numeral 2 identifies a duplet and indicates that the two notes are to be performed in the time normally occupied by three.

Counting the Duplet.   Where the syllables "la" and "li" are used along with the beat number for the natural division in a compound meter, the duplet is performed with the syllable "te" as in a simple meter.

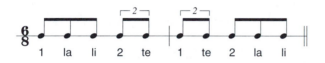

The duplet in a compound meter is performed the same way regardless of the note designated as the beat.

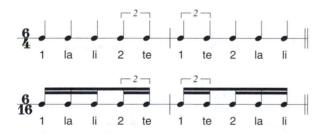

Equivalent Meters

Several possible meters are usually available for a given composition. You have already learned that notation in $\frac{6}{8}$ and $\frac{6}{4}$, for example, or $\frac{3}{8}$ and $\frac{3}{2}$ produces identical performances. Notice, however, that although notated differently, the two passages below containing borrowed divisions will also sound exactly the same.

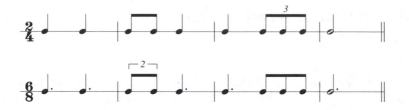

EQUIVALENT METERS are those that have the same accent pattern (the number of beats per measure), but contrasting beat divisions (simple versus compound). The meters $\frac{2}{4}$ and $\frac{6}{8}$ are equivalent; likewise, $\frac{3}{4}$ and $\frac{9}{8}$ are equivalent meters. For any given meter, several different equivalent meters exist. The passage in $\frac{2}{4}$ above could also be transcribed to $\frac{6}{4}$ or $\frac{6}{16}$; both meters are equivalent to $\frac{2}{4}$.

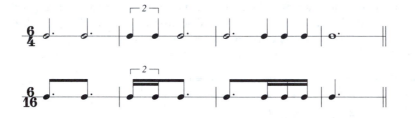

RHYTHMIC READING

I. WARM-UPS

II. EXERCISES

Compare and/or contrast the two solos below in terms of rhythmic content. Your discussion might take the form of a chart or table, a graphic time line, or an analytical paper.

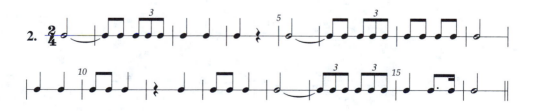

Composition.   Transcription from one meter to another was discussed in Chapter 5. Now, transcribe a rhythmic solo from the original meter to a corresponding *equivalent meter.* When the natural division occurs, a transcription to the equivalent meter will necessitate the borrowed division. Likewise, an instance of borrowed division in the original will be simply the natural division in the transcription. The first solo above, for example, is cast in $\frac{6}{8}$; for an equivalent meter, you might choose $\frac{2}{4}$, $\frac{2}{2}$, or even $\frac{2}{8}$.

SIGHT-SINGING

I. WARM-UPS

In addition to the notation given, practice these passages with alternate possibilities for raised and natural $\hat{6}$ and $\hat{7}$.

The first three warm-ups in minor are preceded by versions in major as you have seen in earlier chapters. As before, compare the two melodies and study the melodic attractions in both modes. Your instructor may direct you to prepare versions in major of other warm-ups, exercises, or studies in this chapter.

II. EXERCISES

Analysis.   Add tempo and performance instructions *in Italian* to the two melodies below. Next, make a detailed reduction of both melodies that shows structural, secondary, and embellishing pitches, prolongations, and roman numeral analysis. Pay special attention to the goal of any accidental present. Speculate, for example, on why the composer employed the raised or natural $\hat{6}$ and/or $\hat{7}$ in light of these goals.

As directed, compare the melodies in the following terms:

a. Melodic motion (conjunct or disjunct).
b. Harmonic basis, including triad outlining, use of seventh chords in the melody, and variety of chords employed.
c. Types of embellishing and other nonharmonic tones employed.
d. The range, tessitura, and contour of the melody.
e. The occurrence of step progressions and/or prolongations.
f. The recurrence of motives and their variation.
g. The form of the melody and an analysis of the melodic cadences.

Allegretto

1.

Allegretto

2.

III. STUDIES

Allegro

1.

Valse

2.

mf

Immer fliessend

3.

f   *ff*   *p*

mf   10

p

Adagietto

4.

mp   2

p

5

p   *mf*   *p*

Andante sostenuto

5.

f

5

mp   1.   2.

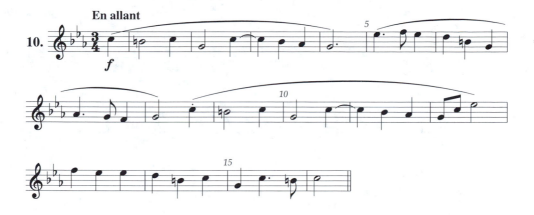

10. En allant

IV. EXCERPTS FROM THE LITERATURE

FRANZ SCHUBERT, *AUFENHALT*
(Abode)

1. Nicht zu geschwind, doch kräftig

SAMUEL BARBER, from *VANESSA*

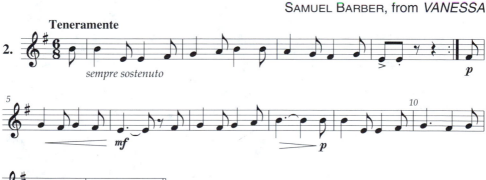

2. Teneramente

L. van Beethoven, Sonata, Op. 13

Bataille, *QUE VEUT CHASSER UNE MIGRAINE*

CLAUDIO MERULO, *WHEN I THINK HOW I LANGUISH*

V. ENSEMBLES

HENRY PURCELL, from *DIDO AND AENEAS*

German Folk Song

SAMUEL BARBER, from *VANESSA*

UNIT FIVE

SECONDARY RESOURCES

Schubert, "Des Müllers Blumen" from *Die Schöne Müllerin*

CHAPTER 10   The Movable C Clefs: No New Rhythmic Material
CHAPTER 11   Secondary Triads: Unequal Triplet Patterns
CHAPTER 12   Secondary Dominants: Augmentation and
                       Diminution

A *Song Cycle* is a group of *lieder* organized loosely around a central programmatic idea. Beethoven is generally credited with having written one of the first song cycles about 1800, but a generation later, by the time Franz Schubert was a mature composer, the *genre* (type of composition) had become an important expression of Romantic ideas through music. *Die Schöne Müllerin* ("The Beautiful Miller Woman") is a cycle of twenty songs composed by Schubert in 1823 and 1824. The songs, on texts by the German poet Müller, center on the theme of first love and present a variety of melodic and harmonic materials. "Des Müllers Blumen" is the ninth song in *Die Schöne Müllerin* and is *strophic* in form—meaning that the two stanzas are sung to the same music.

FRANZ SCHUBERT, DES MÜLLERS BLUMEN
from *DIE SCHÖNE MÜLLERIN*

139

IN UNIT FIVE

Besides the notational systems and primary harmonic materials studied earlier, traditional composers typically used a number of secondary resources. In Chapter 10 you will learn a new clef—the movable C clef that is used in various positions on the staff. "Des Müllers Blumen" is notated here entirely in the alto clef. Because the movable C clefs are new to most students, no additional melodic or rhythmic material is included in Chapter 10.

In previous chapters, you examined the tonic, dominant, and subdominant triads in both major and minor. These diatonic materials are considered primary in the process of establishing a feeling for key. In Chapter 11, however, you will study other diatonic triads that constitute secondary resources: The supertonic, mediant, and submediant triads.[1] These secondary resources provide variety and often serve as substitutes for one of the three primary triads. The supertonic triad outlined in measure 3 of "Des Müllers Blumen," for example, serves as a predominant. Other secondary triads perform similar functions.

In addition to the secondary triads, your study of the borrowed division will continue in Chapter 11 with unequal triplet values.

[1] The leading tone triad, studied in chapter 6 is also a secondary triad.

Few compositions have no pitches at all outside the key. As you have learned, for example, $\hat{6}$ and $\hat{7}$ are often raised in minor. Many accidentals in major and minor keys, however, are the result of secondary function in which the composer creates a new, but *temporary* key center. Secondary function is the central topic of Chapter 12. After you have learned to read in the alto clef, you will note that, while "Des Müllers Blumen" is in the key of A major, the D♯ in measure 8 is introduced as a new, temporary leading tone. Reinforced through the accompaniment, we briefly hear E as a new tonic through a process called tonicization.

In terms of rhythm, Chapter 12 presents a thorough review of all materials studied in the first eleven chapters.

CHAPTER TEN

The Movable C Clefs
No New Rhythmic Material

Allied Theoretical Concepts
■ The Movable C Clefs

Concepts in Pitch: Notation in the C Clefs

Unless you play the viola, the notation of Schubert's "Des Müllers Blumen" on page 139 is probably perplexing. The music is notated not in familiar treble or bass clefs, but in the ALTO CLEF. The alto clef is one of several MOVABLE C CLEFS—so called because the same clef symbol (𝄡) is employed in several different staff locations.

Because the C clefs were used commonly in scores before about 1800, you must read the clefs in order to perform and study the music in older editions. Even in modern scores, the viola, bassoon, cello, and trombone routinely read their parts in one of the movable C clefs.

The C clef "points" to the line that is identified as the pitch C_4 (middle C). Pitches above and below C_4 are identified in the usual manner. Likewise, ledger lines can be used to extend the staff up or down. Viewing only the line for C_4, notice how pitches are notated on the C clef.

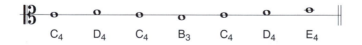

C_4 D_4 C_4 B_3 C_4 D_4 E_4

When the full staff is used, the C clef can appear in four different locations. These clefs are known as SOPRANO, MEZZO-SOPRANO, ALTO, and TENOR respectively. Each clef identifies the position of the pitch C_4.

Soprano   Mezzo-Soprano   Alto   Tenor

C_4 C_4 C_4 C_4

Alto Clef. Although theoretically the C clef may appear on any line, the alto and tenor clefs are the only ones still used in modern notation. The viola, for example, reads its part entirely in the alto clef. The lines on the alto clef are F A C E G; the spaces are G B D and F.

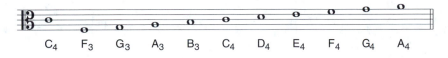

Tenor Clef. The trombone, bassoon, and cello read their parts in both bass and tenor clefs. In the tenor clef, the pitch C$_4$ appears on the fourth line. The lines on the tenor clef are D F A C and E; the spaces, E G B and D.

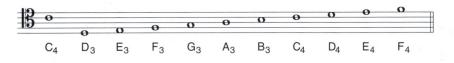

SIGHT SINGING

I. WARM-UP

The first ten exercises can be read in either alto or tenor clef (the pitch names are the same in both clefs, of course). Other exercises follow in both alto and tenor clefs.

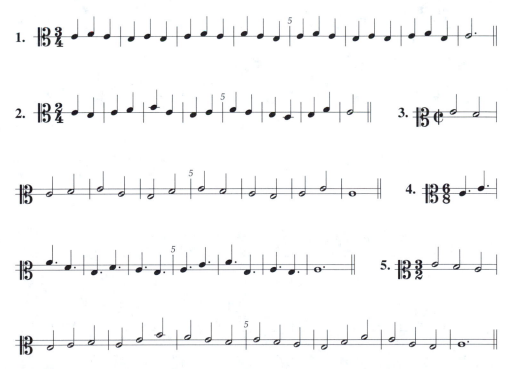

II. EXERCISES

Analysis. As you have done in previous chapters, add performance and tempo indications to the melodies below, which are notated in either alto or tenor clef. Before singing the melodies, conduct a thorough analysis as directed by your instructor.

III. STUDIES

Vif

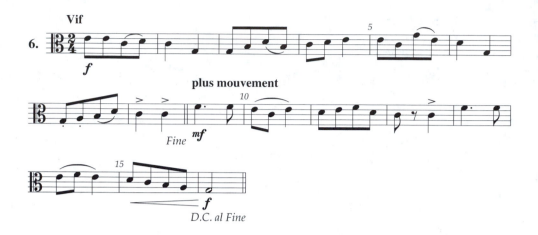

plus mouvement

Fine

D.C. al Fine

Lebhaft

En allant

Adagio

IV. *EXCERPTS FROM THE LITERATURE*

ANNONYMOUS, *IN DULCI JUBILO*

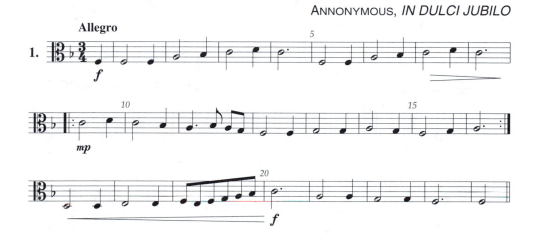

ROBERT SCHUMANN, *AN DEN SONNENSCHEIN*
(Sunshine)

L. van Beethoven, *ADELAIDE*

Larghetto

W. A. Mozart, from *DON GIOVANNI*

Allegro

W. A. Mozart, from *IDOMENEO*

Andante

V. ENSEMBLES

Note that Ensembles 1 and 2 are rounds. The first round is written as a single line; the second ensemble shows the complete score when all three voices have entered.

FRANZ SCHUBERT, *BE WELCOME*

SAMUEL WEBBE, *NOW WE ARE MET*

W. A. Mozart, *DIE ZAUBERFLÖTE*
(The Magic Flute)

Allegro

3.

CHAPTER ELEVEN

Secondary Triads
Unequal Triplet Patterns

Allied Theoretical Concepts
- Diatonic Triads
- Borrowed Division in Simple Meters

Concepts in Pitch: Secondary Triads

Traditional Western music centers on the establishment of a sense of key or tonal center (tonality). Composers create a feeling for key in the mind of the listener through a variety of techniques that balance rhythmic, melodic, and harmonic elements. As you learned in Chapter 5, a progression that involves the primary triads creates a strong sense of tonality. If harmony and melody were limited to these materials, however, music would be predictable. The present chapter is devoted to SECONDARY TRIADS—diatonic possibilities in addition to those termed "primary."

SECONDARY TRIADS

You will recall that there are three functions represented by the tonic, subdominant, and dominant respectively. In addition to these primary triads, the supertonic, mediant, submediant, and leading-tone triads function in a similar way as substitutes. One secondary triad—the leading tone—has already been discussed. The leading-tone triad substitutes for the dominant and typically progresses to tonic. Melodically, $\hat{4}$ moves to $\hat{3}$ and $\hat{7}$ progresses to $\hat{8}$.

Likewise, the supertonic triad can fulfill the "predominant" role of the subdominant as a midpoint between tonic and dominant.

The submediant triad is sometimes used as a substitute for the tonic. The submediant typically follows either the tonic or the dominant. When a progression of dominant to submediant ends a phrase, that progression is known as a DECEPTIVE CADENCE (measures 3–4 below).

The mediant triad is rare. Depending upon the context in which it occurs, the mediant can function in either a tonic or a dominant role.

Chromatic Nonharmonic Tones.   Composers often introduce color into a tonal composition by using nonharmonic tones that are chromatic (that is, outside a given key). Chromatic neighboring tones are especially common in traditional literature. Notice that in the first example below, the D embellishes the pitches E. In the second example, the D♯ creates an even greater emphasis on the diatonic pitch E.

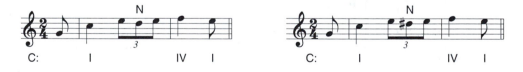

In addition to chromatic neighboring tones, passing tones, appoggiaturas, and other nonharmonic tone types occur chromatically.

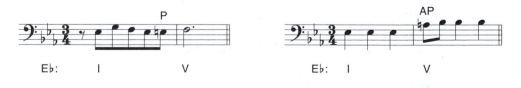

The Escape Tone.   Less common than its opposite (the appoggiatura), an ESCAPE TONE is a nonharmonic pitch that is approached by step and resolves by leap to a consonance. An escape tone typically resolves in the opposite direction to the stepwise preparation.

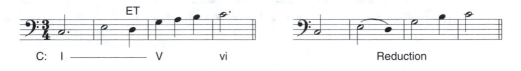

Concepts in Rhythm: Unequal Triplet Patterns

While relatively uncommon, triplet patterns involving rests and unequal values are sometimes found in traditional music. The counting and performance of such patterns parallel those in a compound meter.

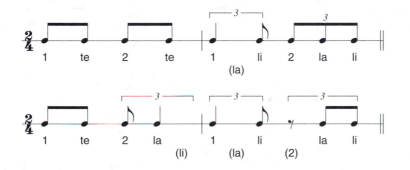

Patterns involving rests in duplet figures are relatively rare in traditional music. Notice, however that the counting syllables used in the theoretical patterns below compare with equivalent patterns in simple meters.

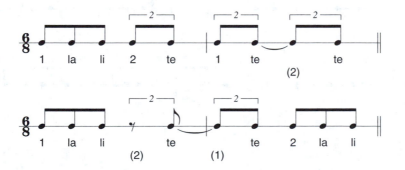

RHYTHMIC READING

I. WARM-UPS

II. EXERCISES

Analysis.   Add tempo and performance instructions *in German* to the solos below. Before performing them, undertake a thorough analysis of the rhythmic content as described in earlier chapters.

SIGHT SINGING

I. WARM-UPS

II. EXERCISES

Analysis.   Add tempo and performance instructions *in Italian* to the two melodies below. Next, before performance, undertake a thorough analysis of one or more of the melodies as directed by your instructor. Consider range and tessitura, the use of sequence, melodic motives and their development, implied harmony, scale forms, melodic cadences, and other areas as appropriate. Make a framework reduction of the melody and identify step progressions.

III. STUDIES

1.

Andante con moto

2.

Andantino

3.

4.

Modéré

IV. EXCERPTS FROM THE LITERATURE

HUGO WOLF, *DAS VERLASSENE MÄGDLEIN*
(The Girl Left Lonely)

JOHANNES BRAHMS, *ABSCHIED*
(Departure)

JOSEPH HAYDN, *RÜCKERINNERUNG*
(Reflection)

GUISEPPE VERDI, from *LA TRAVIATA*

P. I. Tᴄʜᴀɪᴋᴏᴠsᴋʏ, from *EUGEN ONEGIN*

Cᴀʀʟ Mᴀʀɪᴀ Vᴏɴ Wᴇʙᴇʀ, *VARIATIONS ON AN ORIGINAL THEME*

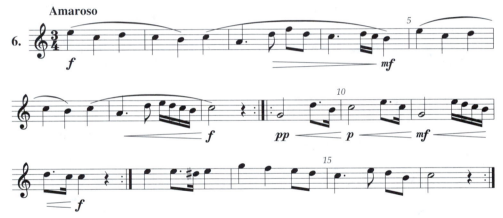

V. ENSEMBLES

The second ensemble (by William Turner) can be sung as a round.

J. S. Bᴀᴄʜ, *NOW THANK WE ALL OUR GOD*
Chorale Harmonization (alto omitted)

WILLIAM TURNER, *HEALTH TO OUR FLEET*

JAMES GREESON, Trio

Secondary Dominants
Augmentation and Diminution

> **Allied Theoretical Concepts**
> - Secondary Function
> - Tonicization
> - Modulation

Concepts in Pitch: Secondary Function

Chromatic pitches in a melody can result either from simple embellishments of diatonic pitches or through the raised $\hat{6}$ or $\hat{7}$ in minor keys. Another source of accidentals in traditional music, however, is secondary function.

PRIMARY FUNCTION is the progressive movement from dominant to tonic in a given key. SECONDARY FUNCTION makes a diatonic triad *other* than the tonic sound temporarily like a *new* tonic—a process termed TONI-CIZATION. In *Des Müllers Blumen* (page 139), measures 1–7 constitute primary function in A major. Secondary function appears in measure 8 with the pitch D♯ creating a temporary new tonic on E. Because E is the dominant of A, the A-major tonality is strengthened by the emphasis on E.

In the example of secondary function above, notice that the dominant triad is preceded by the *dominant of the dominant*. This chord contains the acci-dental D♯, which makes the dominant sound temporarily like a new tonic. The following chords, however, in which D is again natural and in which G♯ ($\hat{7}$) pro-ceeds to A ($\hat{8}$), clarify the old key. Notice that the analytical symbol V/V is un-derstood as "dominant of the dominant."

Modulation and Tonicization.   When a composer moves from one key to another, the music is said to have *modulated*. MODULATION is a relatively permanent key change that will be studied in later chapters. The process sketched above, however, in which the supertonic is heard as a *temporary* new tonic, is tonicization. The supertonic is *tonicized* through the use of its own dominant triad. Any major or minor diatonic triad can be tonicized. When the subdominant is *tonicized* in major, the dominant *seventh* is typically added to provide clarity.

The example below shows various diatonic triads that may be tonicized in major and minor. Notice that some tonicizations are rarely used by traditional composers.

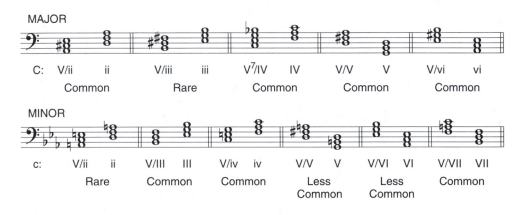

You will observe that the leading tone triad and diminished supertonic in minor are excluded from the examples above. This is because a diminished triad is inherently unstable and cannot be heard as a temporary tonic.

In stepwise passages, the accidental involved in the secondary dominant is often a new leading tone that progresses to the new tonic. If the accidental is a flat (or a sharp made natural) however, it is typically a new fourth scale degree and falls stepwise to the third scale degree.

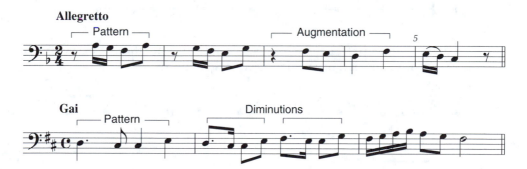

In the first example above, without a knowledge of the harmony, the C♯ might be considered a passing tone rather than part of a tonicization. In the second example, the B♭ is clearly the new fourth scale degree in a tonicization of the subdominant, since other chord tones in V^7/IV are present.

Concepts in Rhythm: Augmentation and Diminution

Composers often begin with an original motive and vary it either by increasing or decreasing the rhythmic values. An AUGMENTATION is a lengthening of the original values; a DIMINUTION consists of a reduction to lesser values. As shown below, rhythmic augmentation and diminution are usually combined with identical or similar melodic patterns. In the first phrase, the original motive is extended through augmentation. The second phrase exhibits the diminution of an idea. Observe that augmentation and diminution may be exact or modified.

RHYTHMIC READING

I. WARM-UPS

These materials constitute a review of all rhythmic problems studied in Parts I–IV of this text.

These patterns include syncopations and should be performed on a single pitch instead of on successive scale degrees.

II. EXERCISES

Add tempo and performance instructions *in Italian* to both of the rhythmic solos below.

Composition.   Choose one of the solos above and compose two variations based on the rhythms of the original. Center one of the variations on similar rhythmic ideas in an equivalent meter (a solo in $\frac{6}{8}$ might be varied in $\frac{2}{4}$ or $\frac{2}{2}$, for example). In the second variation, use the original meter, but center the variation on an augmentation or diminution of an important motive. Include performance instructions and indications of tempo *in Italian* and strive for accurate and legible calligraphy.

SIGHT SINGING

I. WARM-UPS

The passages below include the tonicization of various diatonic triads in major and minor. While a tonicization typically returns quickly to the original key, many of these brief passages terminate with the new tonal area. Be sure to analyze the implied harmonies before you perform the warm-ups.

II. EXERCISES

Add performance and tempo indications *in French* to the two melodies below. Before performing them, make a harmonic reduction, highlighting any instances of secondary function.

Composition.   Compose an original melody for voice or an instrument as directed by your instructor. Limit your harmonic and melodic vocabulary to those materials studied thus far in the text. If you encounter difficulties beginning the solo, you might choose one of the melodies above, one of the studies, or an example from the literature as the harmonic and/or stylistic basis of your original composition. Do not however, make your melody a variation; while you might follow a pre-existing rhythmic or harmonic plan, the melodic ideas should be your own. Your instructor may also ask you to prepare an analysis of the melody. Use the following guidelines:

   a. The form should be a double period of four phrases.
   b. Use at least one implied dominant seventh chord in the melody with the seventh itself resolving appropriately.

c. If writing for voice, use conjunct motion predominantly. If the melody is for an instrument, more disjunct motion may be appropriate, but be certain that you remain within the instrument's range.

d. Include two different secondary dominants with the accidentals appearing in the melody and resolving characteristically.

III. STUDIES

Andante semplice

Allegro e ben marcato

Allegretto

Andante expressivo

4.

più mosso

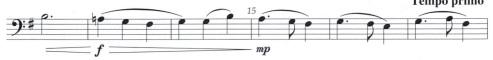

Fine *mp*

Tempo primo

D.C. al Fine

Larghetto

5.

p

Andante

6.

sfz *mp*

Andante cantabile

7.

Ziemlich schnell

8.

Andante piacevole

9.

IV. EXAMPLES FROM THE LITERATURE

Chorale Melody, *BEFIEHL DU DIENE WEGE*
(Command Thy Way)

Wilhelm Taubert, *IN DER FREMDE*
(In A Strange Land)

JOHANNES BRAHMS, *DER SCHMIED*
(The Blacksmith)

JOHANNES BRAHMS, *MINNELIED*
(Love Song)

JOSEPH HAYDN, *MASS IN TIME OF WAR*
(Gloria)

JOHANNES BRAHMS, *SOMMERABEND*
(Summer Evening)

V. ENSEMBLES

ANTONIN DVORAK, *MORAVIAN DUETS*

ROBERT SCHUMANN, *SPANISCHES LIEDERSPIEL*
(Spanish Song-Play)

HENRY PURCELL, from *DIDO AND AENEAS*

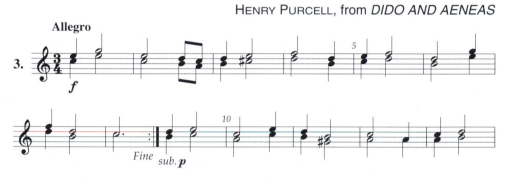

SIMPLE MODULATION

W. A. Mozart, *Daphne deine Rosenwangen*

Wolfgang Amadeus Mozart (1756–91) is considered one of the greatest Western composers. Mozart lived during the Classical Era (ca. 1750–1825) when music was typically symmetrical, not especially chromatic, and composed both for professional and amateur musicians. Together with his contemporary, Joseph Haydn (1732–1809), Mozart created symphonies, string quartets, concertos, and other masterworks of instrumental literature that are still revered today.

In addition to such major works, however, Mozart, like other composers, wrote simple songs with piano accompaniment, such as *Daphne deine Rosenwangen*. These songs were appropriate for performance at public concerts and recitals, but they were also within the grasp of many amateur performers. As the general public in Europe increased its appreciation of great music after about 1725, composers like Mozart and Haydn were able to supplement their salaries as court composers with royalties from published works. While both Haydn and Mozart earned their livings primarily by serving as court composers, the next generation, which included Beethoven (1770–1827), were able to support themselves entirely through royalties, teaching, commissions, and subscription concerts. Simple works like *Daphne deine Rosenwangen* remained popular throughout the nineteenth century and, in fact, are still in vogue with artists and profitable for publishers today.

W. A. Mozart, *DAPHNE DEINE ROSENWANGEN*
(Daphne, All Thy Radiant Beauty)

IN UNIT SIX

You will recall that tonicizations are but temporary tonal shifts. In Unit 6 you will find that compositions often include modulations—changes of key center that redefine the tonality. In Chapter 13, you will learn that modulations can be either closely or distantly related. You will further encounter three types of modulations and learn how to differentiate among them.

Chapter 14 centers on modulations that are less closely related to an original tonic. The method employed for modulation is central in the effectiveness of the key change.

In terms of rhythmic studies, both chapters of this unit center on two-part performance. No new rhythmic material appears in Unit 6.

CHAPTER THIRTEEN

Modulation to Closely Related Keys
Two-Part Studies—Simple Meters

Allied Theoretical Concepts
- Modulation
- Closely Related and Distantly Related Keys

Concepts in Pitch: Closely Related Keys

When composers change keys in a composition, they often choose a key that is closely related. A CLOSELY RELATED KEY is one that differs by no more than one flat or sharp from another given key. If keys are not closely related, they are DISTANTLY RELATED. Given the key of C Major, for example, the keys that are closely related are shown below:

Keys Closely Related to C Major

| A Minor (Relative Minor) | F Major | D Minor | G Major | E Minor |

Using a closely related key for a modulation has the advantage of smoothness, since the two keys differ by only one pitch. Modulations to distantly related keys, on the other hand, are often shocking to the listener, since few pitches may be in common.

TYPES OF MODULATION

In general, there are three different types of modulation: *common chord, chromatic,* and *phrase.* While in this text the accidental that effects the key change is usually in the melody, this is not always the case in the literature. Accidentals may occur in the harmony under or over a melody that appears entirely diatonic in the old key. This fact makes analysis and the selection of an appropriate pivot pitch crucial.

Common-Chord Modulation.   The link between keys in a common-chord modulation is one chord that is diatonic in both the old and the new keys. The common chord usually has predominant function in the new key and progresses respectively to the new dominant and the new tonic.

While a chord of predominant function is often used as a pivot chord in modulations, such is not always the case. In Mozart's *Daphne deine Rosenwangen,* the common chord in the modulation from A major to E major is not the subdominant in the new key, but rather the tonic (measure 6). When the key returns to A major, the pivot chord is again the new dominant (measure 19).

The Pivot Pitch.   When a melody modulates, you must begin hearing pitches in the new key at some point. The choice of the *pivot pitch* is important. Quite often, the modulation will involve an accidental in the melodic line. In this case, the pitch *preceding* the accidental will serve as a melodic pivot point (as in the passage above).

If an accidental does not appear in the melody the choice of a mental point of redefinition may be less obvious. In *Daphne deine Rosenwangen,* accidentals that facilitate the modulation appear in the accompaniment—not the melody. The change occurs long before the first accidental in the melody (measure 13). In the return to A major, the process is reversed: $\hat{5}$ in E major becomes $\hat{2}$ in the original key. Again, the key change occurs without accidentals in the melody.

Chromatic Modulation.   In a CHROMATIC MODULATION, there is no common chord; the link between the two keys is an ascending series of three half steps heard typically in the same voice. The second and third pitches of the series are $\hat{7}$ and $\hat{8}$ respectively in the new key; the first pitch is a chromatic half step below the second.

If $\hat{7}$ in the new key is a diatonic pitch in the old key (a modulation to the subdominant in major, for example), the chromatic line descends. The second and third pitches are the new $\hat{4}$ and $\hat{3}$ respectively. The first pitch is a chromatic half step above the second.

Phrase Modulation.   A type of key change often referred to as PHRASE MODULATION usually involves a strong cadence in the old key. After a pause or other dramatic gesture, the new key begins immediately. In a phrase modulation, the link between the two keys is through formal design. One phrase ends; the next phrase begins in a new key.

Concepts in Rhythm: Performing Two-Part Studies

In earlier chapters you have performed ensembles as duets, trios, and so on. In the present chapter, however, while there is no new rhythmic material, your task is to perform both parts of a duet simultaneously. Begin with a thorough analysis of each duet, then sing both parts individually using the method specified by your instructor. Next, sing or tap one part as written while tapping the beat, beat division, or beat subdivision (as appropriate for the second part). Finally, choose a slow tempo and perform both parts as written.

RHYTHMIC READING

I. WARM-UPS

The warm-ups in this chapter are in two parts. At least three methods of performance are appropriate:

a. Tap one part with the right hand and the other part with the left hand.
b. Sing one part on a single pitch using counting syllables while tapping the second part.
c. Sing one part as a scale (major or one of the three forms of minor). The second part should be tapped or clapped. Note: Both parts are not appropriate for scale performance. The part that might be sung as a scale is marked with the word "Scale." This part is based on a repetitive rhythmic figure as seen in earlier chapters. The second part is often more varied.

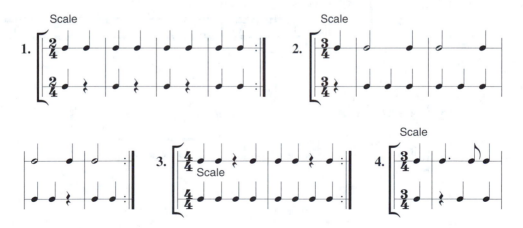

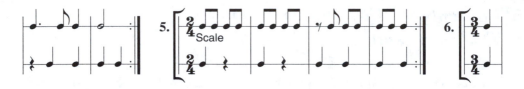

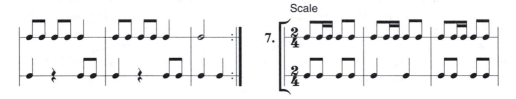

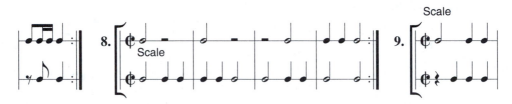

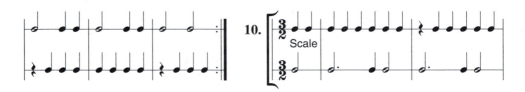

II. EXERCISES

Analysis.   Two duets follow for analysis and performance. First, add tempo and other appropriate instructions *in German*. Before performing the exercises, undertake an analysis of each part. You may analyze parts separately as you have done in previous chapters. When considering the parts together, however, take special note of the following:

    a. Are any rhythmic motives present in both voices? Are there instances of the augmentation or diminution of motives in either or both parts?

    b. Is one part predominant, or are the two parts more or less equal in importance?

    c. Is there a difference in the range of rhythmic values used in the two parts? Does one part feature any special characteristics (rests, for example).

The second duet includes a simple melodic line as well as a part to be performed rhythmically. Sing the melody as directed by your instructor, and tap or clap the lower part at the same time.

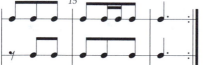

SIGHT SINGING

I. WARM-UPS

While you have only the implied harmony available, speculate on the type of modulation employed in each warm-up (common chord, chromatic, or phrase). Locate an appropriate pivot pitch and mark this point with scale-degree numbers in both the old and new keys ($\hat{3}$ in F major = $\hat{5}$ in D minor, and so on).

5.

6.

7.

8.

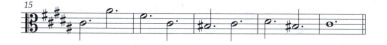

II. EXERCISES

Analysis.   Add tempo and performance instructions *in Italian* to the exercises below that include modulation. In your analysis, consider the following:

- a. What are the old and new keys? Do any accidentals present constitute new leading tones or new fourth scale degrees?
- b. Speculate on the method of modulation employed (with the melody alone, this may not be clear).
- c. Which pitch in the melody serves as a pivot to the new key? Which (if any) facilitates a return to the old key?
- d. How substantial is each key area? About the same? Does one dominate?
- e. Does the modulation affect the formal plan?

As directed by your instructor, analyze the melodies in terms of structure, step progressions, formal plan, range, and other areas of investigation studied earlier.

III. STUDIES

Tempo primo

D.C. al Fine

Allegro con spirito

4.

Modéré

5.

Fine

D.C. al Fine

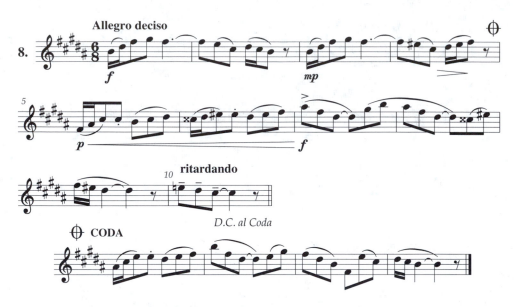

8. Allegro deciso

IV. EXCERPTS FROM THE LITERATURE

W. A. MOZART, *MASS IN C MAJOR (CREDO)*

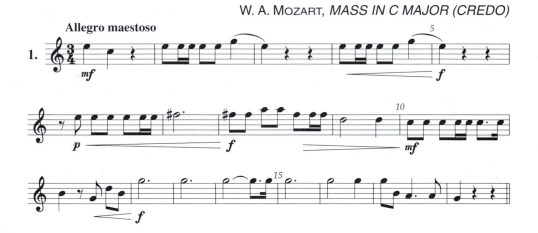

Allegro maestoso

W. A. MOZART, *DAS TRAUMBILD*
(A Vision)

2. Ruhig

G. F. HANDEL, "Thou shalt Bring Them In"
from *ISRAEL IN EGYPT*

GUSTAV MAHLER, *RHEINLEGENDCHEN*
(Rhein Legends)

ROBERT SCHUMANN, "Wenn ich in diene Augen seh' "
(When I Look into Your Eyes) from *DICHTERLIEBE*

FRÉDÉRIC CHOPIN, *MÄDCHEN'S WUNCH*
(Maiden's Wish)

V. ENSEMBLES

Innig

1.

Fine

zurückhalten

D.C. al Fine

L. van Beethoven, *CONSTANCY*

Andante ed expressivo

2.

HENRY ALDRICH, *TOM JOLLY'S NOSE*
18th-Century English "Catch" (Round)

CHAPTER FOURTEEN

Modulation to Distant Keys
Two-Part Studies—Compound Meter

Allied Theoretical Concepts
- Closely Related and Distant Keys
- Modulation and Tonicization
- Types of Modulation
- Change of Mode

Concepts in Pitch: Distant Keys

You learned in the previous chapter that two keys differing by no more than one sharp or flat are termed "closely related." Other key relationships are known as DISTANT. Keys which are distantly related to C major, for example, are all of those *except* A minor, F major, D minor, G major, and E minor (those that are closely related). The keys of D major and D♭ major, for example, are both distant to C major.

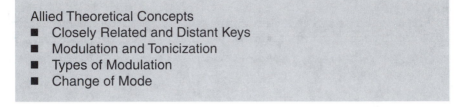

C Major   D Major   D♭ Major
Distantly Related Keys

Remote Keys. While both D major and D♭ major are keys distant to C major, they are not equal in their respective degrees of distance. The key of D major has five pitches in common with C major (D, E, G, A, and B) while D♭ has only two (F and C). Further, while C major and D major have two diatonic triads in common (E-G-B and G-B-D), there are no common chords between C major and D♭ major. The relationship between keys such as C major and D♭ major, where no diatonic triads are in common, is termed REMOTE. Modulations are possible from one key to any other given key, but when composers modulate to remote keys, they often use special pivot chords with chromatic and/or enharmonic interpretations. These techniques of modulation will be studied throughout the next several chapters.

Conventional Modulations to Distantly Related Keys

The fact that two keys are distant does not preclude a common chord modulation. As we have seen, from C major, five keys are closely related and can be reached through common-chord modulation. In addition, the keys of B minor, G minor, D major, and B♭ major all have at least one chord in common with C major.

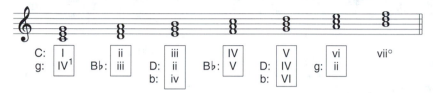

C:	I		ii		iii		IV		V		vi	vii°
g:	IV[1]	B♭:	iii	D:	ii	B♭:	V	D:	IV	g:	ii	
				b:	iv			b:	VI			

While a chord of predominant function in the new key is usually preferable as a common chord, any of the chords shown above could serve as the pivot in a modulation.

Chromatic Modulation.   In addition to several distant keys available through common chord modulation, other tonal areas can be reached through the chromatic link. A modulation from C major to E♭ major, for example, can be accomplished smoothly by using the chromatic process described in the previous chapter. Because $\hat{7}$ in E♭ major (D) is a diatonic pitch in C major, the chromatic line descends through $\hat{4}$ and $\hat{3}$ in the new key. The first note of the three-pitch series is a chromatic half step above the second and is harmonized in the old key. Notice that in the example below, the new $\hat{4}$ and $\hat{3}$ are harmonized with the new dominant seventh and tonic respectively.

[1]This relationship assumes raised $\hat{6}$ in G minor.

Phrase Modulation.   Composers often employ phrase modulation between remote keys. The process is exactly the same as described earlier with keys that are closely related: A phrase ends in the old key; another begins in the new key. Remote phrase modulations are often more striking and effective than similar modulations between closely related keys.

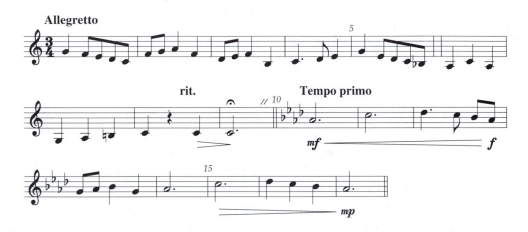

Change of Mode

The term "key" is defined as the sensation in the mind of the listener that *one pitch* is more important than any of the others. Given this definition, if we begin in C major and move to C minor, we have not modulated since the tonic is still the same. A shift from C major to C minor is described as a CHANGE OF MODE or a MODAL SHIFT. Modal shifts provide color within the original tonality and have been common in traditional music since about 1700. Remote modulations using change of mode as a pivot chord will be discussed in the next chapter.

Concepts in Rhythm: Performing Two-Part Studies

Review the instructions for performing two-part studies on page 189. The present exercises center on the beat, beat division, and beat subdivision in compound meters.

RHYTHMIC READING

I. WARM-UPS

Perform the two-part passages below as you did the similar exercises in the previous chapter. If the problems prove difficult, practice the two parts separately. As before, the part that can be performed as a scale passage is marked with the word "scale."

7.

8.

9.

10.

11.

12.

II. EXERCISES

Add tempo and performance instructions *in English* to the two-part solos below. Before performing them, undertake a thorough analysis of the rhythmic content as described in earlier chapters.

Composition.   Compose an original two-part composition that is appropriate for rhythmic performance. The composition should be in the form of a double period using either of the plans shown below.

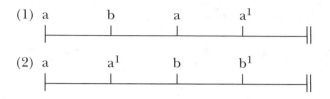

(1) a   b   a   a¹

(2) a   a¹   b   b¹

Begin by composing a number of different rhythmic motives. Choose the one that you feel is most interesting and compose the upper line using a motivic structure that reflects your chosen formal plan. Next, compose the lower part as a complement to the upper. Remember that the two lines of the composition are to be performed by the same musician, so be careful to avoid complicated rhythms.

Make the score complete in terms of tempo and performance instructions (use *Italian*). Number the measures and be sure to align beats between the two parts.

SIGHT SINGING

I. WARM-UPS

These passages include modulations both to closely related and distant keys. Make a careful analysis of each study before you perform it.

II. EXERCISES

Add performance and tempo instructions *in French* to the exercises below.

Composition.   Compose an original melody in D major that modulates to the dominant, then returns to the original tonic. Begin by choosing a formal plan for a double period (see pages 36 and 210 for suggestions). Be careful to adhere generally to melodic attractions in the respective keys. Choose either a common-chord or a chromatic modulation and employ the appropriate accidentals in the melody. Compose the first period so that the first phrase establishes D major and modulates to A major in the second phrase. Begin the second period in the dominant and return in the fourth phrase to the original key.

III. STUDIES

Adagietto

3.

Marcato

Fine

ff

D.C. al Fine

Larghetto

4.

f

sub. *p*

Herzlich

5.

mf

mit empfindung

p

mf

Andantino

6. *f* *mp*

stendando

f

D.C. al Coda

CODA

mf

Flowing

7. *mp*

mf *f* *p*

slower to end

mf

Allegro vivo

8. *f*

L'istesso tempo

ff *f*

IV. EXCERPTS FROM THE LITERATURE

FRANZ SCHUBERT, *MORGENLIED*
(Morning Song)

Ziemlich langsam

J. S. BACH, *JESU MEINE FREUNDE*
(Jesus, My Friend)

L. Zaneti, *ARREZZATI, MIO CORE*
(Stop, My Heart)

Franz Schubert, *JÄGERS LIEBESLIED*
(Hunter's Lovesong)

JOHANNES BRAHMS, *VORSCHNELLER SCHWUR*
(A Vow Made in Haste)

V. ENSEMBLES

Throughout the seventeenth century, Western composers used a type of abbreviated notation called *Figured Bass*. The numbers under the bass in the chorale below indicate how the alto and tenor voices should be added. Your instructor may want you to complete the harmonization according to Bach's specifications. In addition, the soprano and bass voices alone can be sung as a duet.

GOTTFRIED VOPELIUS, *SEI GEGRÜSSET*
(Hear My Pleading) Harmonization by J. S. Bach

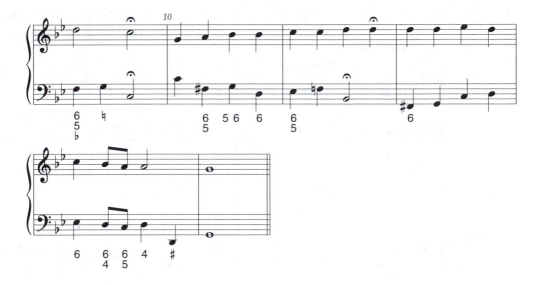

JOHANNES BRAHMS, *LOVE SONG WALTZES*

J. S. Bᴀᴄʜ, *ERMUNTER DICH, MEIN SCHWACHER GEIST*
(Awaken, My Weak Spirit)

UNIT SEVEN

CHROMATIC RESOURCES

Johannes Brahms, *Komm Bald*

The period of Common Practice Harmony extends roughly from 1600 to 1900. Even before 1875, however, composers began reaching for the limits of the tonal system. Chopin, for example, is known for bold chromatic experiments and innovative uses of nonharmonic tones. Other composers, like Schubert, began with the traditional diatonic relationships among triads and found ways to retain basic functions, yet impart chromatic interest.

JOHANNES BRAHMS (1833–97), a German, lived during the Romantic Era (ca. 1825–1900)—the beginning of a transitional period that eventually brought an end to tonality as it had been practiced by Bach, Mozart, and even Beethoven. Brahms is remembered today as a master of most Romantic forms and *genre*, including *lieder*. Like Schubert and Schumann, Brahms wrote *lieder* that expressed not only Romantic notions of love and other human emotions, but that also tapped the full range of nineteenth-century harmonic idioms.

Komm bald (Come Soon!) is a brief work in ternary (ABA) form. The middle section (measures 15–28) illustrates one way in which composers like Brahms employed familiar chords to achieve smooth modulations to distant keys. The song begins in A major; as we would expect, the first modulation is to the dominant (measures 11–14).

In the middle section, however, a diminished-minor (borrowed) supertonic seventh chord in measure 18 begins a modulation to F major (strengthened by the emphasis on the dominant in measures 21–24). While the modulation to F is gradual, the return is striking as the listener *retroactively* reinterprets the tonic in F major as a Neapolitan in E major (measures 26–28).

Like other innovative composers in the nineteenth century, Brahms exploited familiar relationships to effect smooth, but rapid modulations between distant keys. In the case of *Komm bald*, a rich texture is created through simultaneous nonharmonic tones (see the first few measures of the piano accompaniment below). Although the tonal plan itself is simple, borrowed chords, a Neapolitan employed as a pivot, and the interweaving nonharmonic tones create an illusion of harmonic ambiguity.

JOHANNES BRAHMS, *KOMM BALD*
(Come Soon!)

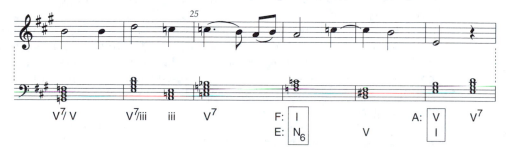

IV   ii   V⁷   I

IN UNIT SEVEN

In Chapter 15, you will encounter a number of traditional resources used to extend the tertian system. Some of these techniques, like various types of seventh chords, were common as early as the seventeenth century. In addition to the dominant seventh chord already studied, several other qualities of seventh chords exist. Further, you will study chordal sevenths not only on the dominant, but on most other diatonic triads as well.

In addition to seventh chords, traditional composers used other sonorities that include chromatic alterations. These materials include borrowed chords that blend pitches between major and parallel minor, as well as altered chords of predominant function.

In terms of rhythmic studies, Chapter 15 includes exercises in less common meters and values. While meters like $\frac{3}{4}$ and $\frac{6}{8}$ were the norm in the Common Practice Period, in earlier music you will encounter meters like $\frac{2}{1}$, in which the whole note receives the beat. Twentieth-century composers, on the other hand, have favored meters like $\frac{4}{8}$ and $\frac{3}{16}$. While all such meters can be reduced to familiar accent patterns and beat divisions, the notation may appear unusual and difficult at first. The studies in Chapter 15 are designed to familiarize you with these less common meters.

Especially in the Romantic Era, composers used enharmonic relationships to modulate to remote keys. A number of these relationships will be surveyed in Chapter 16. Like the Brahms excerpt on page 224, an enharmonic relationship depends upon the listener's ability to hear a single chord as functional in two different keys. Using these enharmonic relationships, composers devised ingenious ways to lead the listener smoothly into distant key areas.

To this point, you have studied symmetrical meters: those that are constructed of *either* duple or triple groupings. An *Asymmetrical Meter* is one in which each measure has at least one duple pattern *and* at least one triple pattern. Asymmetrical meters, especially quintuple ($\frac{5}{4}$, $\frac{5}{8}$, and so on), became increasingly common in the last half of the nineteenth century and continue to be employed frequently by composers today.

CHAPTER FIFTEEN

Extended and Altered Diatonic Harmony
Less Common Meters and Values

Allied Theoretical Concepts
- Root-Position and Inverted Seventh Chords
- Augmented Sixth Chords
- The Neapolitan Six
- Third Relation

Concepts in Pitch: New Diatonic and Chromatic Resources

Even from the time of J. S. Bach (1685–1750), two supplements to basic diatonic harmony were common: seventh chords and altered chords of subdominant function. Both of these categories will be discussed in this chapter.

Seventh Chords

You have already learned about root-position and inverted dominant seventh chords. You should be aware, however, that with the exception of the tonic, traditional composers routinely added sevenths to other diatonic triads.[1] Seventh chords are classified according to (1) the quality of the triad, and (2) the quality of the seventh. The dominant seventh chord, therefore, can also be identified as a "major-minor" seventh.

In major keys, diatonic seventh chords occur in four qualities: "major-major" (usually termed "major"), "major-minor" ("dominant"), "minor-minor" ("minor"), and "diminished-minor" (known as "half-diminished"). Observe the qualities of the various seventh chords shown below in B♭ major. Notice also that the ø symbol is used to indicate the relative instability of the leading-tone seventh.

---

[1]If a seventh is added to the tonic, the chord becomes unstable and therefore generally ceases to be heard as a tonic. A seventh chord that actually *functions* as a tonic is very rare in Common Practice music.

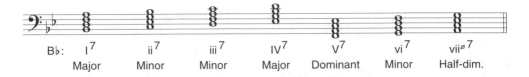

Bb: I⁷   ii⁷   iii⁷   IV⁷   V⁷   vi⁷   viiᵉ⁷

Major   Minor   Minor   Major   Dominant   Minor   Half-dim.

Inversions of all seventh chords are identified just as inverted dominant sevenths are.

Bb: V$_6^5$ ii$_4^3$ vii$^{ø}_2^4$

One additional quality of seventh chord arises from minor: Diminished-diminished (known as "fully diminished" or just "diminished"). This chord occurs as an extension of the leading tone triad. In analysis, the circle symbol appears with a fully diminished seventh chord.

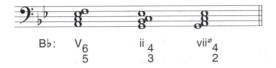

g: vii°⁷   vii°$_5^6$

Singing Seventh Chords.   Complete seventh-chord outlines are relatively rare in the literature. More often, the melody includes one or two of the chord tones with the full chord appearing in the harmony. From the melody alone, in fact, it may be impossible to differentiate tones of a seventh chord from other, more simple melodic patterns. The seventh itself, however, almost invariably resolves down by step to a consonant tone in the next chord.

Mit hastig

7th

7th

C: viiᵉ⁷   I   IV   V^7/V   V

Nondiatonic Seventh Chords.   Especially in the nineteenth century, compositions in major keys often included "borrowed" chords that were actually diatonic in the parallel minor. The half-diminished supertonic seventh, for example, and the fully diminished leading tone seventh (diatonic in minor) often appear in major keys and provide additional color.

Borrowed Chords

A change of mode from major to parallel minor (or the reverse) creates no tonal disorientation. Accordingly, traditional composers often employed BORROWED CHORDS—diatonic triads in minor, for example, that are used in a major key. As previously discussed, vii°₇ used in major constitutes a type of borrowed chord.

Other borrowed chords are common. In G major, a minor subdominant creates no tonal ambiguity because the root is the same and the chord is typically followed by the dominant.

Brahms often employed borrowed chords—both for color and for their value in modulations. In measure 18 of *Komm bald* (page 225), the half-diminished (rather than minor-minor) supertonic seventh begins a modulation that eventually reaches F major. Notice in the passage below that while the seventh of the chord (A) is followed by the third and root respectively, the first pitch in measure 19 is G♯ and constitutes a regular resolution of the seventh.

Altered Chords of Predominant Function

A second class of extended diatonic harmony involves several "cliché" chords with curious designations like "Neapolitan six" and "German Augmented Sixth." These chords involve altered subdominants that resolve typically to the dominant and therefore actually strengthen the feeling for key rather than weaken it. Altered chords are rarely outlined melodically in their entirety, but their traditional resolution in a melodic context sometimes results in awkward intervals like the diminished third.

Augmented Sixth Chords.   A full discussion of augmented sixth chords lies outside the scope of a sight-singing text. Suffice it to say that each chord contains the interval of an augmented sixth that expands to an octave and emphasizes $\hat{5}$ in both voices (harmonized typically with V or i$^6_4$).

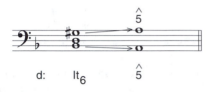

The three common versions of the augmented sixth chord are shown below. Origins of the geographic names are obscure, but the "Italian" and "German" versions of the chord are based on a minor subdominant triad with raised root. Notice that the "French Sixth," which is a half-diminished seventh chord with raised third, is in second inversion. All three chords are the same in major and minor.

In melodies, the upper pitch of the augmented sixth ascends by half step; the lower pitch descends by half step. In the so-called "Italian Augmented Sixth," for example, the melody may include either pitch of the augmented sixth interval (or those pitches may be in the harmony).

Misterioso

Neapolitan Six.   The NEAPOLITAN SIX (a major triad in first inversion and built upon lowered $\hat{2}$) is not technically a borrowed chord. Because traditional composers resolved the Neapolitan six to the dominant (or tonic six-four), however, it belongs with the augmented sixth chords in the category of altered predominant harmony. The Neapolitan six is the same in major and minor.

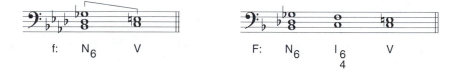

When N_6 resolves to the dominant, lowered $\hat{2}$ descends melodically to $\hat{7}$; this diminished third is often in the melody.

Brahm's use of a Neapolitan six in *Komm bald* (measure 26) is not exceptional as a strong and colorful cadence formula in E major. The C-natural, fifth of the Neapolitan, appears in the soprano and is held over to form a 9-8 suspension as the chord resolves to the dominant. Another aspect of this passage, the use of the Neapolitan six as a pivot chord, will be discussed in Chapter 16.

Altered Mediants.   A mediant relationship refers to chord roots a third apart. More specifically, however, the term connotes a root movement by third *with a cross relationship* between the two chords (an E in one chord and an E♭ in the next, for example). In the nineteenth century, composers began to employ ALTERED MEDIANTS in which the mode is changed from major to minor or the reverse. Sometimes the mediants are "borrowed" from the parallel major or minor (an E♭ major triad used in C major, for example). In other cases, the altered mediant has no relationship with the parallel key and is used simply for its colorful effect (an A major triad in C major). Both of these possibilities are shown in the example below.

Concepts in Rhythm: Less Common Meters and Values

As discussed in the introduction to Unit 7, traditional composers only occasionally employed meters with a whole- or sixteenth-note beat. These meters, however, are common before and after the Common Practice Period. When you encounter unusual meters, remember that the counting will be exactly as it would be performed in a more common meter.

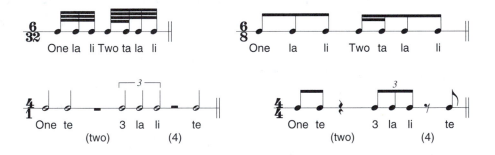

RHYTHMIC READING

As you have done previously, perform these warm-ups as scales, with counting syllables, or on a neutral syllable.

I. WARM-UPS

These warm-ups include syncopations and are not easily performed as scales. Play these exercises on an instrument or use counting or other syllables.

Two-Part Studies

Perform these passages as you did earlier. You might sing one part on a neutral syllable and tap the other, tap both parts with right and left hands, or play one part on a single pitch on the piano while singing or tapping the other part.

II. EXERCISES

Analysis.   Two exercises follow for analysis and performance. Add tempo and other appropriate instructions *in Italian*. Prior to performance, analyze the two parts. In addition to an analysis of the parts separately, consider their effect together as well. See page 191 for potential areas of analysis.

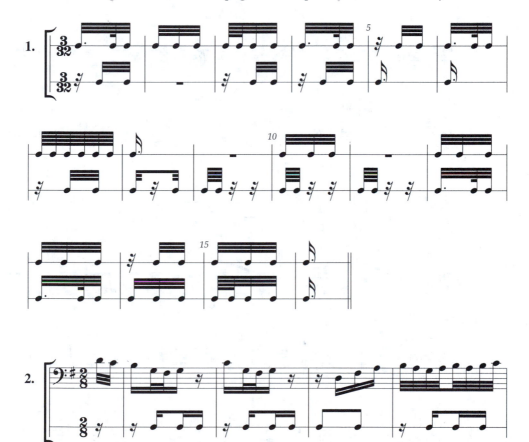

SIGHT SINGING

I. WARM-UPS

II. EXERCISES

Analysis.   Two melodies follow for analysis. Add performance and tempo instructions *in French*. Then, prior to performance, write a brief analytical paper comparing and contrasting the two melodies in some or all of the following areas (as directed by your instructor):

   a. Length, formal design, and use of motives (sequence, variations, repetition, and so on)
   b. The range, contour, and tessitura.
   c. The use of implied seventh chords or change of mode (if any).
   d. The use of secondary function and/or altered chords (if any).
   e. The type of modulation employed (if any) and the relationship between the two tonal areas.

III. STUDIES

Grave

1.

Lebhaft

2.

Trés vif

3.

Allegretto

4.

Più mosso

Pastorale

5.

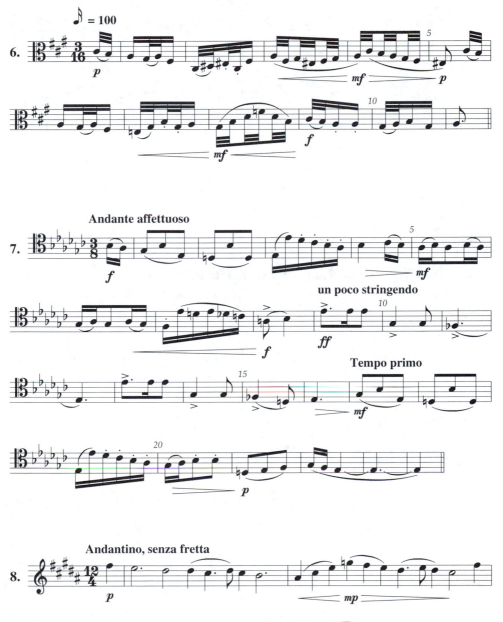

IV. *EXCERPTS FROM THE LITERATURE*

W. A. Mozart, *EVENING SONG*

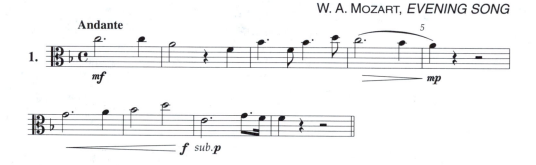

Franz Schubert, *GESTÄNDNIS*
(Confession)

AMY BEACH, *MEDOW-LARKS*

GIOVANNI BONONCINI, *LA SPERANZA I CORI AFFIDA*
(Hope Sustains the Heart)

W. A. Mozart, *SECRET LOVE*

FRANZ SCHUBERT, *THE MILLER AND THE BROOK*

V. ENSEMBLES

FRANZ SCHUBERT, from Mass in E♭ Major

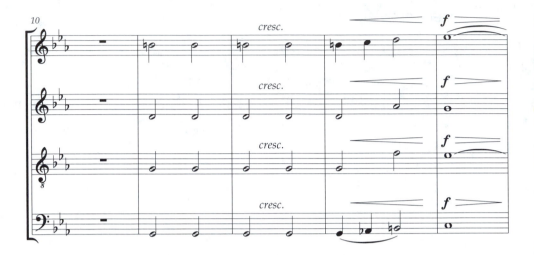

L. van Beethoven, *THE HEAVENS ARE TELLING*

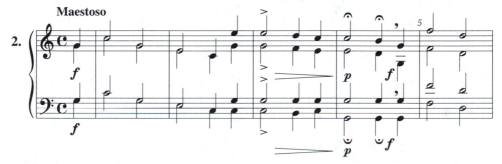

JOSEPH HAYDN, from Mass in B♭ (Agnus Dei)

CHAPTER SIXTEEN

Chromatic and Enharmonic Principles
Asymmetrical Meters

Allied Theoretical Concepts
- Enharmonic Modulation
- Asymmetrical Meters

Concepts in Pitch: Enharmonic Relationships

As the nineteenth century progressed, many composers were increasingly intrigued with enharmonic and chromatic possibilities. In addition to borrowed and other chords used simply for their color, diminished sevenths, the German six-five, and the Neapolitan six, among others, facilitated modulation to remote keys.

Enharmonic Diminished Seventh Chords

Fully diminished seventh chords were common in traditional music from at least 1700. In G minor, for example, vii°₇ resolves to i; regardless of the notated inversion, $\hat{7}$ ascends typically to $\hat{8}$ and $\hat{4}$ descends to $\hat{3}$.

The tendencies just discussed are shown in the phrase below.

Because the fully diminished seventh chord is made up entirely of minor thirds, inversions are impossible to discern aurally. Composers exploited this aural ambiguity to effect modulation to remote keys. Any pitch of the diminished seventh chord, for example, can be heard as the root; accordingly, at least four different functional resolutions are possible for any one chord. Hearing the diminished seventh, the listener assumes a typical resolution as shown below.

If an enharmonic alternate resolution is followed by appropriate harmonic choices, however, modulation to a remote key can be smooth and effective.

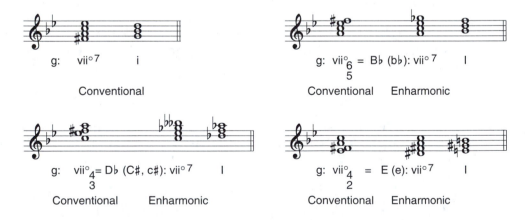

As is often the case in traditional music, the complete diminished seventh chord may not be arpeggiated in the melody. Volatile pitches such as $\hat{7}$ or $\hat{4}$ may appear in the melodic line; other pitches may be supplied in the harmony. In enharmonic modulations, composers typically spell chords according to their functions in the new key.

The German Six-Five/Dominant Seventh Relationship

By the mid-Baroque (ca. 1675), the German six-five, discussed in the previous chapter, was a common altered subdominant used to provide color in a traditional resolution to tonic six-four. Listeners heard the familiar German six-five and anticipated the regular resolution (see page 230).

Traditional composers were aware, however, that the German six-five is indistinguishable aurally from a root-position dominant seventh chord:

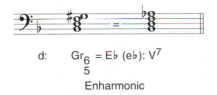

If the German six-five in the example above resolves to tonic six-four, its role is clearly predominant. If, on the other hand, the German six-five were reinterpreted enharmonically as a dominant seventh chord and resolved to tonic, it is heard retroactively as a chord of dominant function. Composers often used this enharmonic relationship to modulate up or down by minor second.

The Neapolitan Six/Dominant Six Relationship

Some composers in the nineteenth century used the Neapolitan six, another Baroque-Era color chord, as an effective enharmonic pivot. While the Neapolitan six is typically used in a predominant role, like any major triad, it has potential dominant function.

The Neapolitan six resolves typically to dominant or tonic six-four.

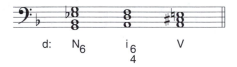

d: N_6 i_6^4 V

Enharmonically, the Neapolitan six can be heard and interpreted as a first-inversion dominant triad in the key a tritone higher or lower. For the listener to perceive this new role, however, a chord of tonic function must follow the dominant.

g: i N_6 V

Traditional

g: i N_6 $D\flat: V_6$ V^7 I

Enharmonic

In addition, composers used the Neapolitan in its traditional role as a predominant. Discussed earlier, Brahms created a smooth modulation from F major to E major in his lied, *Komm bald* (see page 224). The listener hears an F major triad in two different roles: first as the tonic (measure 26), and two measures later, retroactively as the Neapolitan in E major.

F: V^7

E: $\begin{array}{c}I\\N_6\end{array}$ V   I

Singing Melodies With Enharmonic Relationships.   Analysis is crucial in singing melodies that include enharmonic relationships. Study the score closely to determine where modulations occur; this will determine the point at which you begin to hear and feel scale degree tendencies in the new key. If the melody is to be sung at sight, the analysis must be done mentally as you sing.

Concepts in Rhythm: Asymmetrical Meters

An ASYMMETRICAL METER is one that includes at least one duple and at least one triple accent pattern. Even before the 1850s, some composers employed asymmetrical meters for variety and to achieve special rhythmic effects. Although less common than duple, triple, and quadruple meters, asymmetrical metric schemes appear in the music of nineteenth- and twentieth-century composers. As are more conventional meters, asymmetrical patterns like $\frac{5}{4}$, $\frac{7}{4}$, $\frac{5}{8}$, and $\frac{15}{8}$ are either simple or compound, and they are counted just as other meters are.

One complexity associated with asymmetrical meters is the uneven division of the measure (accent pattern). In $\frac{5}{4}$, for example, the measure can be divided either as $2 + 3$ or $3 + 2$.

Teneramente

In $\frac{7}{8}$, the measure might be divided $3 + 4$, $4 + 3$, or even $2 + 2 + 3$. Notice that beams can be used to clarify the division of the measure.

Scherzo

In modern works, composers who choose asymmetrical metric plans often use dotted barlines to specify the division of the measure.

Moderato

     Especially in the twentieth century, composers have expressed asymmetrical groupings with a meter signature such as $\frac{2+3}{4}$ or $\frac{3+2}{8}$. This choice eliminates the need for divided measures as the accent pattern is clarified in the signature itself.

Doucement

RHYTHMIC READING

Due to the nature of asymmetrical meters, these warm-ups should be performed with counting syllables or other means instead of scale patterns.

I. WARM-UPS

Two-Part Studies

Perform both parts of these studies simultaneously. Sing one part while tapping another, tap both parts, or perform one part on an instrument and sing or tap the other.

II. EXERCISES

Analysis.   The two rhythmic studies below are asymmetrical in their metric construction. Prior to performance, add tempo and other instructions in the language of your choice. In your analysis of one or both of these studies (as directed), concentrate on the metric structure and the motivic development.

a. Is the duple/triple accent division clear? Is this division consistent throughout the melody? If changes in accent division occur, does this change affect the form of the melody (Is one phrase 2 + 3 with another divided 3 + 2, for example)?

b. Are phrases constructed from one motive in a duple pattern and another in a triple pattern? Does one division of the measure predominate?

c. Do single motives span both a duple and a triple pattern?

d. How are motives developed? How does the asymmetrical structure affect motivic development?

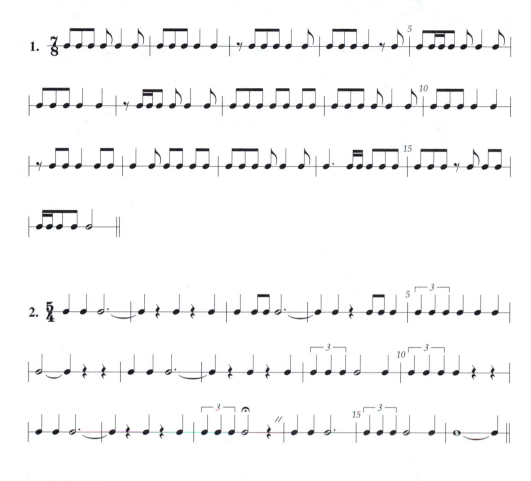

SIGHT SINGING

I. WARM-UPS

Prior to performance, make a careful examination of the implied harmonies, including pivot chords that facilitate modulations. Next, choose the *pitch* in each modulation that will begin tonal associations in the new key.

II. EXERCISES

Add performance and tempo instructions *in German* to the melodies below. Each of the melodies modulates either through a simple diatonic relationship or a more complex enharmonic connection. Identify the type of modulation, the key relationships, the use of accidentals, and other aspects of melodic construction as you did previously (see page 194).

Composition. Compose a melody that modulates through an enharmonic relationship. Use a double period form and consider writing a brief introduction to the melody (see Study 5 in this chapter). Before beginning your composition, plan the harmony and harmonic rhythm. Next, create a number of rhythmic motives in different meters and choose the best one or two of these.

As a next step, choose pitches that complement the rhythmic motive(s). If the rhythms are intricate, pitch repetition might be appropriate; a slower-moving motive, on the other hand, might need more frequent pitch changes. Finally, develop the motive(s) into full phrases and periods. Be attentive to melodic contour and balance.

III. STUDIES

Before you sing these melodies, make an analysis of the implied harmonies including any remote modulations. Pay particular attention to potential pivot pitches.

4. Tempo di tarantella

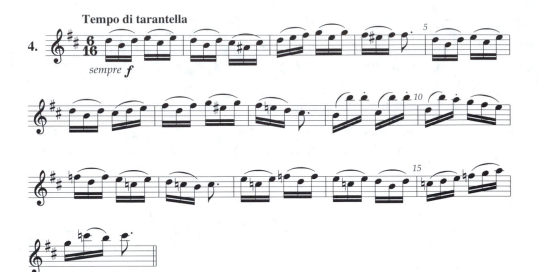

sempre **f**

5. Adagio   Allegro con brio

6. Modéré et doucement

7.

8.

IV. EXCERPTS FROM THE LITERATURE

LEONARD BERNSTEIN, *CHICHESTER PSALM 108*

ANTONIN DVORAK, from *STABAT MATER*

HECTOR BERLIOZ, *L'ILE INCONNUE*
(The Unknown Island)

FRANZ SCHUBERT, *SEHNSUCHT*
(Longing)

L. van Beethoven, *VOM TODE*
(Death)

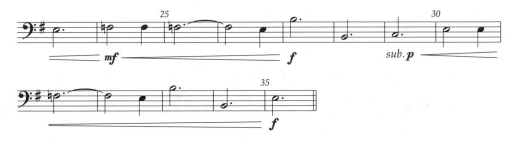

V. ENSEMBLES

James Greeson, *À Trois*
(Trio)

RICHARD WAGNER, from *LOHENGRIN*

NONTRADITIONAL TONAL RESOURCES

James Greeson, *Exultate*

At first, the lines of *Exultate* may seem ordinary enough. Although the meter changes frequently, the rhythms themselves are straightforward. At first glance, you will notice that the piece is cast in a three-part (ABA) form with an imitative section forming the middle material. You will further observe, however, that while the composition begins in A minor, the subtonic (G) is is used frequently. Many composers at the beginning of the twentieth century rediscovered melodic materials that had been popular before the Baroque Era, but which had been disregarded by Common Practice Composers. *Exultate* begins in the Aeolian mode—one of the Medieval Church Modes, and what today we call "natural minor." While traditional composers would have employed a leading tone (G♯ in this case), Greeson retained the subtonic which imparts the characteristic flavor of the Aeolian mode.

JAMES GREESON,[1] *EXULTATE*

[1]James Greeson (b. 1951) is an associate professor of Composition and Music Theory at the University of Arkansas in Fayetteville. He received his doctorate in composition from the University of Wisconsin and MM and BM degrees from the University of Utah. Many of his compositions have been recorded and published by Galaxy Music, Cor Publishing, Willis Music, the UNC Jazz Press, and See Saw Publishers. He is also active as a jazz and classical guitarist and is an avid scuba diver.

poco più mosso

IN UNIT EIGHT

In modern use, the Church Modes can be described as whole- and half-step series similar to major and minor scales. In fact, the Aeolian mode seen in the
beginning of *Exultate* is a precursor of the minor scale. In Chapter 17, you will
study the Church Modes and learn new diatonic patterns that were common in
music before 1600 and after about 1875.

Two-part rhythmic studies continue in this chapter with an emphasis
on solos that have more frequent rests, ties, and syncopations. Some of the
studies will also include the borrowed division in simple or compound meters.

Alongside new melodic materials like the modes, composers in the
early twentieth century employed a wide range of techniques within the framework of tonal harmony. Some of these, like modal scales, are rooted in traditional functional progressions, while others that you will study, like the
octatonic scale (the middle section of Greeson's *Exultate*), result in harmonies
without traditional tendencies.

In Chapter 18, you will study and sing melodies created by composers who wrote in varied styles, yet had at least one common aim: The establishment of a new music that would provide an alternative to the Romantic-Era vocabulary of composers like Tchaikovsky, Brahms, and Mahler.

Mixed meters have no consistent duple, triple, or quadruple accent pattern, like the meters you have encountered thus far. Seen in *Exultate,* and common in the late nineteenth and early twentieth centuries, mixed meter avoids traditional metric patterns. You will learn in Unit 8 that mixed meters are of two types: those, as in *Exultate,* in which the unit of beat remains constant (beat = beat), and others in which the pulse changes (beat ≠ beat). The latter category of mixed meters will be explored in Chapter 18.

CHAPTER SEVENTEEN

The Church Modes
Two-Part Studies—Ties, Rests, and Syncopations

Allied Theoretical Concepts
■ The Church Modes

Concepts in Pitch: New Melodic Resources

In addition to major and minor, composers in the late nineteenth and early twentieth centuries looked toward a number of new melodic materials to add color to their tonal music. One group of such resources is the Church Modes. While music of the Common Practice Period typically employed a leading tone (even in minor) and is referred to as *tonal,* music before 1600 and some music after about 1875 is described as MODAL because most of the scale forms feature a subtonic rather than a leading tone.

THE CHURCH MODES

The earliest Western music was based on four series of half and whole steps called MODES.[1] Named DORIAN, PHRYGIAN, LYDIAN, and MIXOLYDIAN respectively, the four Authentic Church Modes are shown below transposed to begin on the pitch C. Like scales, modes span an octave.

Dorian Mode   Phrygian Mode

---

[1]Technically, the modes were eight in number although a study of the four "Plagal" forms lies outside the scope of this text.

Lydian Mode   Mixolydian Mode

By 1550, two additional modes were common in Western music. The AEOLIAN MODE is the same as what we now call the natural minor scale. The major scale was originally known as the IONIAN MODE.

Aeolian Mode   Ionian Mode

Major and Minor Characteristics.   Modes are classified as either major or minor. Dorian and Phrygian are minor modes because the distance between the first and third pitches is a minor third (as found in Aeolian or natural minor). Likewise, Lydian and Mixolydian can be categorized as major since the first and third degrees are separated by a major third.

Notice the differences between the minor modes and the natural minor scale (Aeolian mode).[2]

Aeolian Mode	Natural Minor Scale
Dorian Mode	Natural Minor Scale with raised $\hat{6}$
Phrygian Mode	Natural Minor Scale with lowered $\hat{2}$

The simple melody below is cast first in natural minor (Aeolian), then in Dorian and Phrygian modes respectively. Like natural minor, Dorian and Phrygian modes have a subtonic.

Minor Melody (Aeolian)

Dorian Melody

Phrygian Melody

---

[2]Another minor mode, termed Locrian, will be discussed in the next chapter as a synthetic scale.

Similar observations can be made about the major modes and their relationships to the major scale.

Ionian Mode	Major Scale
Lydian Mode	Major Scale with raised $\hat{4}$
Mixolydian Mode	Major Scale with lowered $\hat{7}$

Study and sing the three melodies below. The first is major (Ionian), the second Lydian, and the third is Mixolydian. Observe that Major and Lydian have leading tones, while the Mixolydian scale includes a subtonic. While the pitch names remain the same, the modal inflections are reflected in the key signature.

Melodic Attractions. Your success in singing functional modal melodies will be enhanced if you know the inherent melodic tendencies exhibited in the six melodies shown above. Remember that melodic tendencies are strongest following a leap. In each of these six modes, $\hat{1}$, $\hat{3}$, and $\hat{5}$ are stable pitches. In the Phrygian mode, lowered $\hat{2}$ has a strong tendency to descend to 1; in other modes, this attraction is common, but somewhat weaker.

In all of the modes except Lydian, $\hat{4}$ has a strong attraction to $\hat{3}$ just as it does in major or minor. In Lydian, the raised $\hat{4}$ has a weak attraction to $\hat{3}$.

In natural minor (Aeolian), $\hat{6}$ typically descends to $\hat{5}$; in the other modes, $\hat{6}$ has a weak tendency depending upon the ultimate goal of the passage.

Finally, as has been discussed previously, in any scale or mode, a leading tone retains its strong attraction to the tonic. The subtonic usually moves in a similar, but weaker manner if the goal of the passage is the tonic. If $\hat{5}$ is the goal, the subtonic usually descends.

Accidentals.   Just as a composition in C major may employ a number of accidentals yet remain solidly in the original key, accidentals are not uncommon in modal melodies. As you have done in other chapters, analyze the melody to determine whether an accidental is embellishing or structural. Embellishing pitches will be associated musically with the tone emphasized. An accidental that is a structural pitch will often function as a new leading tone or new fourth scale degree.

Concepts in Rhythm: Two-Part Exercises

Continue your study of two-part performance with passages that incorporate rests, ties, and syncopations. Follow the guidelines for two-part practice and performance given in Chapter 13 (page 189).

NOTES ON RHYTHMIC NOTATION

The notation of Western music has changed through the years and even today varies from one country to another. In addition, music editors often disagree on the best notation for a given passage. The indication of a duplet, for example, might appear in two different ways:

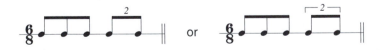

Another duplet notation is fairly common (especially in older French editions). This notation is equivalent to the more modern duplet pattern.

The notation above also appears in triple-simple meters where two notes of equal value fill a measure. Most contemporary music editors prefer the second notation below, however, since it emphasizes the triple accent pattern.

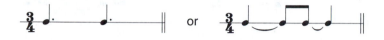

Triplets with various markings abound in the literature. All three patterns below are equivalent in value.

PRACTICE VERSIONS

Especially with melodies that include complex rhythms (ties, syncopations, borrowed division, and so on), you may first want to construct a simplified, practice version. In creating a practice version, consider some or all of the following:

- a. Insert notes in the place of rests.
- b. Eliminate ties.
- c. Convert borrowed divisions to the natural division.
- d. If necessary, rewrite the passage with notes of equal value (based on the smallest value in the line).

Once you have mastered the practice version, add (or delete) ties, rests, borrowed divisions, and other complexities gradually until you are performing the music as written. The passage below shows how the first four measures of Exercise #2 on page 282 might be rewritten for practice. Other performance problems might be addressed with different simplifications.

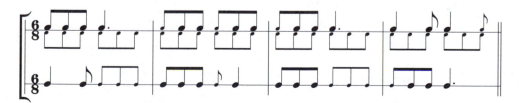

RHYTHMIC READING

I. WARM-UPS

1.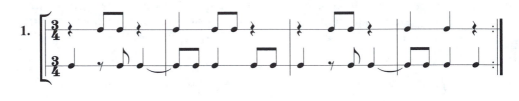

2.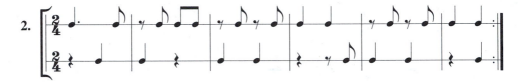

3.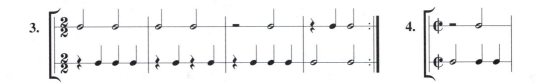

4.

5.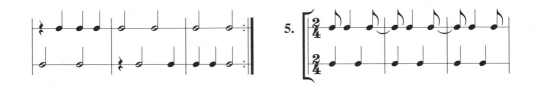

6.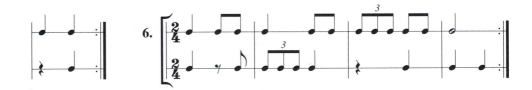

II. EXERCISES

Analysis. The two passages that follow (as well as the warm-ups above) feature various two-part rest, tie, and syncopated patterns. Before performance, write simplified, practice versions of the two-part studies for your own use. You can do this by adding notes in place of rests, eliminating ties, and renotating syncopated patterns. Through this activity, you will also be analyzing the music and any displacement of beats. Write new versions of both parts and practice these before moving on to the original notation.

This exercise includes a vocal line in Dorian mode. Sing the upper part while tapping the lower line.

SIGHT SINGING

I. WARM-UPS

Before practicing the warm-ups below, sing complete ascending and descending modes (see pages 275 and 276) on a variety of tonics.

The key signatures of the modal warm-ups below identify a particular mode. In practice, however, you may perform them in any mode by adding sharps or flats to the key signature. Notice how the changes in key signature shown below alter the mode with E as the tonic. Study these relationships and be prepared to alter the mode of any of the warm-ups at sight.

Major   Lydian   Mixolydian

Minor   Dorian   Phrygian

II. EXERCISES

Add tempo and performance directions *in French*. Next, study the melodies below and determine the melodic structure.

Composition. Write a melody that, like those above, is based on a modal scale (other than Aeolian or Ionian). Make the melody a double period in form with the phrase structure of your choice. Use this melody as the basis of a variation that is based on a different mode. If your original melody is Lydian, for example, your variation might be Phrygian or Mixolydian. You might also change the meter and/or texture of the variation. Add tempo and performance directions in the language of your choice.

III. STUDIES

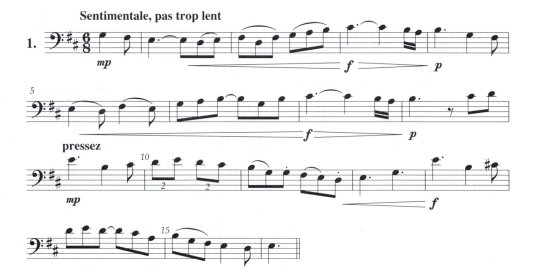

Largo sostenuto

3.

stringendo

Schnell

4.

Fine

D.C. al Fine

Allegro marziale

5.

Andante

8.

IV. EXCERPTS FROM THE LITERATURE

English Folk Song

Andantino

1.

MARCO DA GAGLIANO, *PUPILLE ARCIERE*
(The Simple Archer)

Allegretto

2.

ANDREA FALCONIERI, *DONN' INGRATA*
(Ungrateful Lady)

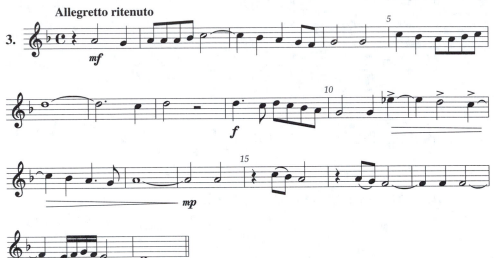

CLAUDE DEBUSSY, *L'ISLE JOYEUSE*
(The Joyful Island)

MAURICE RAVEL, Quartet in F

V. ENSEMBLES

13th-Century German Carol

CLAUDIO MONTEVERDI, Madrigal

César Franck, *LA VIERGE À LA CRÈCHE*
(The Virgin at the Crib)

3.

Andante e tenero

CHAPTER EIGHTEEN

Nontraditional Melodic Resources
Mixed Meters I—Beats Equivalent

Allied Theoretical Concepts
- Pandiatonicism and Nonfunctional Harmony
- Quartal Harmony
- Ninth Chords
- Synthetic Scales
- The Whole Tone and Pentatonic Scales

Concepts in Pitch: Nontraditional Materials

At the turn of the century, while composers like Mahler and Strauss remained content with the traditional tonal vocabulary, others began searching for new melodic and harmonic materials. Arnold Schoenberg (1874–1951), for example, founded a completely new music that was systematically atonal. Others, like Debussy, Scriabin, Hindemith, and Prokofiev, remained faithful to the theory of tonality, but found ways to make their music distinctive and innovative. This latter category of early twentieth-century musical style is the focus of the present chapter.

NEW MELODIC RESOURCES

In addition to the Church Modes discussed in the last chapter, a number of additional scale forms either originated in the late nineteenth and early twentieth centuries or were rediscovered by the composers of that era. Some of these materials, like the Locrian mode, have melodic attractions similar to those found in major and minor; others, like the whole tone scale, are new resources devoid of traditional tonal tendencies.

SYNTHETIC SCALES

In the last decade of the nineteenth century, several composers experimented with original scale forms. Scales that do not fall into one of the standard categories (Major, Dorian, harmonic minor, and so on) are termed SYNTHETIC.

Claude Debussy (1862–1918) was a French composer who had a special fondness for a scale that combines the raised $\hat{4}$ of Lydian and the subtonic from Mixolydian. On the other hand, Béla Bartók, Igor Stravinsky, and others often used an OCTATONIC SCALE—one that has eight pitches and is constructed of a series of alternating whole and half steps. Also favored by Bartók and others is the "Hungarian" scale which includes two augmented seconds.

Lydian/ Mixolydian   Octatonic   Hungarian

The middle (B) section of Greeson's *Exultate* (page 271, measure 17) is based upon the octatonic scale. An ascending tetrachord forms the motive for a brief passage of imitative counterpoint. The tenor begins the octatonic series on G; the alto enters with the fifth pitch (C♯), and the soprano's first pitch (G in measure 19) completes the scale. Notice that the interval of imitation is a tritone. While this relationship was traditionally approached cautiously or avoided entirely, it has been popular in this century among composers like Greeson.

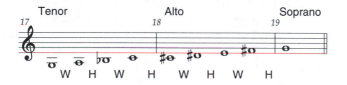

Melodies based on synthetic scales often involve unusual intervals that pose performance problems. As always, locate the tonal goal of a passage and relate other pitches to that goal. You may want to eliminate all but structural pitches and gradually add back tones that at first may seem difficult. The next melody, for example, is based on a synthetic scale. The practice version represents a progressive step toward mastery of the original passage.

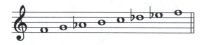

Original passage

Practice version

The Locrian Mode.   You may have noticed that, including Aeolian and Ionian, traditional modes occur as white-note series beginning on C, D, E, F, G, and A. Because the dominant pitch was so important in early modal theory, the white-note series built on B, termed the LOCRIAN mode, was only a theoretical possibility. In Locrian, the interval between $\hat{1}$ and $\hat{5}$ is an unstable diminished fifth. Keep in mind, however, that composers are not committed to any one scale or any one tonality throughout a composition. A work might begin in Locrian on G and modulate to natural minor or Dorian on E, for example.

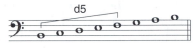

Locrian Mode

While Common Practice composers found the Locrian mode unacceptable, it constituted a new synthetic scale resource for more innovative composers in the twentieth century. The melody below is based on Locrian transposed to E. While $\hat{2}$ has a strong attraction to $\hat{1}$, and $\hat{4}$ progresses naturally to $\hat{3}$, (lowered) $\hat{5}$ often falls to $\hat{4}$ with $\hat{3}$ as the ultimate goal.

The Whole-Tone Scale

A six-note series closely associated with Claude Debussy is the WHOLE-TONE SCALE. Intervals between adjacent pitches in the whole-tone scale are all major seconds. The seventh pitch is the enharmonic equivalent of the first.

Whole Tone Scale

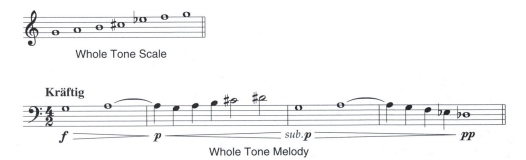

Whole Tone Melody

The Pentatonic Scale

A scale that predates the Church Modes by many centuries is a five-note series known as the PENTATONIC SCALE. There are several forms of the pentatonic scale; the one most often seen is equivalent to a major scale with $\hat{4}$ and $\hat{7}$ removed.[1]

Pentatonic Scale

Lacking $\hat{4}$ and $\hat{7}$—the pitches with the strongest tendencies—pentatonic melodies are often nonfunctional. Tonality is established through repetition, accent, or harmonic implications. Many folk melodies from both the Eastern and the Western worlds are pentatonic. Notice that both "Camptown Races," an American folk tune, and "Arilang," a Korean folk song, are pentatonic.

"Camptown Races" (Western)

"Arilang" (Korean)

NEW HARMONIC MATERIALS

Some new melodic ideas of the twentieth century are harmonically based. NONFUNCTIONAL harmony or melody, generated through a number of different materials and techniques, is defined by its lack of the traditional melodic attractions ($\hat{4}$—$\hat{3}$ or $\hat{7}$—$\hat{8}$, for example). In addition to the nonfunctional music of late nineteenth- and early twentieth-century composers, you will find works in this chapter from the Middle Ages and Renaissance. Except for modes, introduced in the previous chapter, music outside the Common Practice Era has been excluded thus far because it does not typically conform to the melodic attractions that were emphasized in chapters 1–16. You should be thoroughly familiar with tonal singing at this point, however, and ready to explore new melodic patterns.

---

[1]While the pentatonic scale is compared here with the major scale as a pedagogical aid to singing, the pentatonic predates the major scale and is constructed theoretically from a series of perfect fifths.

Pandiatonicism

When a melody remains within a given scale system (major, Dorian, and so on), yet does not adhere to traditional tonal attractions, that melody is said to be PANDIATONIC. If a melody is pandiatonic, any tone in the scale system can precede or follow any other tone. Chromatic embellishments, however, typically conform to expected tendencies so as to preserve the character of the scale: sharps tend to ascend by step while flats descend. Pandiatonic melodies are customarily tonal, but the tonality is established through means apart from traditional melodic tendencies: Repetition, accent, harmonic plan, and so on. Further, the tonal center in a pandiatonic work may change frequently.

The following passage from Greeson's *Exultate* is pandiatonic in Aeolian on A (measures 9–11) and ends similarly in E♭ major, but without traditional melodic tendencies. Notice that in both phrases, not only is a leading tone absent, but $\hat{4}$ rarely falls to $\hat{3}$. Finally, observe that Greeson chose E♭ (and not E) as a second point of tonal emphasis in the passage. This same tritone relationship was discussed earlier in reference to the middle section of the composition.

Extended Tertian Harmony

While most Common Practice composers were content with tertian triads and seventh chords, adding an extra third above the seventh to form a NINTH CHORD was not unknown even as early as the eighteenth century.

Complete ninth chords are rarely outlined in a melody, and the melodic interval of a ninth is itself fairly rare. The ninth is most recognizable when a seventh ascends by third within the same chord and then descends. Stepwise motion from a seventh may signal a ninth as well, but without access to any accompaniment, you may not be able to differentiate implied ninth chords from other tonal materials.

Chromaticism

While chromaticism in some form has been a part of Western music virtually since its beginning, late nineteenth- and early twentieth-century composers used it in new ways. Synthetic scales and whole-tone passages are easily categorized. Other uses of chromaticism, however, are more individual and are idiosyncratic to particular composers and schools.

A group of influential Russian composers in the early 1930s, for example, created a style that has been (perhaps erroneously) termed "wrong-note harmony." A melody in this style will move along in a given major or minor key for several measures, then divert to a distant key for a few beats before returning to the original tonality.

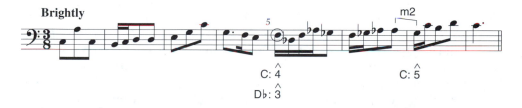

While the phrase above is striking, the performance problems are hardly new. "Wrong-note harmony" and other, similar chromatic shifts should be approached like any other key change: Through analysis of the pivot notes into and out of the new key.

Quartal Harmony

The essence of Common Practice music is tertian harmony (superimposed thirds), but composers in the late nineteenth century experimented with other harmonic systems. QUARTAL HARMONY is based on the perfect fourth. Quartal triads have an open, slightly dissonant sound that appealed to composers like Paul Hindemith (1895–1963) and the American Charles Ives

(1874–1954), as well as Debussy and Stravinsky. Quartal harmony, while typically tonal, is nonfunctional. Melodic patterns often center on major seconds and perfect fourths in combination. You will want to approach a quartal melody first by analyzing the stepwise scale patterns as well as any familiar tertian structures. Next, isolate and practice intervals that defy traditional tendencies. The tonal center in a quartal work may change frequently and abruptly.

The following melody combines a quartal flavor with chromatic embellishment and occasional tertian patterns.

Concepts in Rhythm: Mixed Meters

Among several Medieval concepts to find favor in the late nineteenth century is mixed meter. Where a metric structure like $\frac{3}{4}$ or $\frac{9}{8}$ creates a sense of security, alternating meters may generate an unbalanced rhythm that generates momentum and increases listener interest. When meters alternate throughout a composition, the pulse in one meter may be retained for the second meter (equivalent beats).[2]

Simple equivalent beat (beat = beat) mixed meter is exhibited in the line below. The basic pulse is the quarter note. When the meter changes to $\frac{2}{4}$, and later to $\frac{3}{2}$, there is no interruption in the flow of the beat, although the number of quarter notes per measure changes. The pulse of the quarter note remains constant throughout as indicated by the marking ♩ = ♩.·

When you practice a passage with mixed meters, you may find it helpful to sketch a constant pulse that is appropriate for the given passage. Set the metronome to this pulse or tap it with one hand while singing the rhythms. Notice how the passage below might be clarified to facilitate an accurate performance.

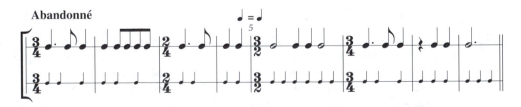

---

[2]When the dotted-quarter in $\frac{6}{8}$ is equal to the quarter note in $\frac{2}{4}$ (♩· = ♩), the beats are equivalent (beat = beat). Meters with nonequivalent beats will be discussed in the next chapter.

RHYTHMIC READING

I. WARM-UPS

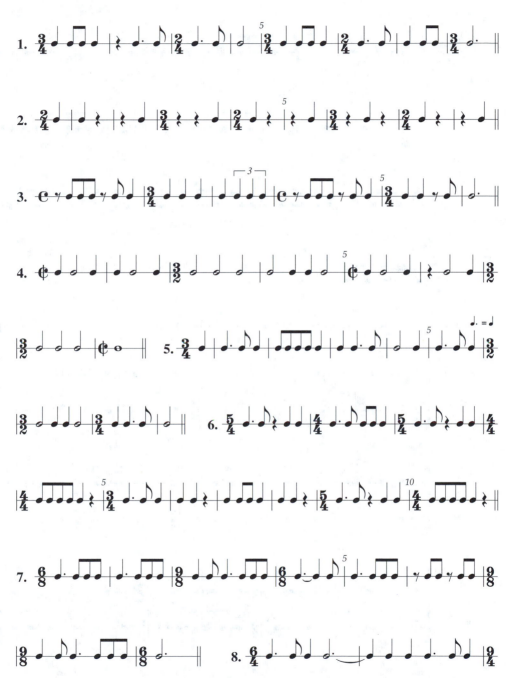

These two-part exercises should be performed as in previous chapters.

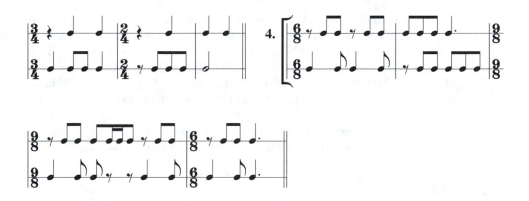

II. EXERCISES

Add tempo and performance instructions *in German* to the solos below. Before performing them, undertake a thorough analysis of the rhythmic content as described in earlier chapters (see pages 50, 191, and 256).

Composition. Compose a duet for two percussion instruments that features mixed meter, where the unit of beat is constant (or where the unit of beat in one meter can be heard as a multiple of the beat in the other meter ($\frac{3}{4}$ and $\frac{4}{2}$, for example). The duet should be at least thirty-two measures in length and might be successfully structured as two double periods forming a binary or AB form. Create interesting rhythmic ideas, but make sure that you include sufficient contrast to retain the listener's interest over the entire composition.

Include tempo and performance instructions in the language of your choice. Copy the music carefully and include measure numbers.

SIGHT SINGING

I. WARM-UPS

The following warm-up passages are based on many different melodic resources. If the music is constructed from a synthetic or other exotic scale, you may want to write and practice the scale before attempting the patterns involved.

These warm-ups are pentatonic.

The following warm-ups are based on synthetic scales. First, analyze the melody to determine the pitches in the scale. Remember that some pitches may be embellishing and that some scales may have more or fewer than seven discrete pitches. On a separate sheet, notate and practice the scale before performing the warm-ups.

These melodies are whole tone in construction.

The following warm-ups are quartal, pandiatonic, or include nontraditional chromatic passages.

II. EXERCISES

Analysis.   Two melodies follow for analysis and performance. Begin by adding tempo and other instructions *in English*. Next, determine the scalar basis for each melody and make a thorough analysis of motives, form, use of sequence, cadences, and other areas as you have done in previous chapters. If directed to do so, complete a graphic reduction showing prolongations, embellishing tones and so on. Locate and mark step progressions as well as any unique feature of the melody.

III. STUDIES

a tempo

Moderato

7.

Avec mouvement

8.

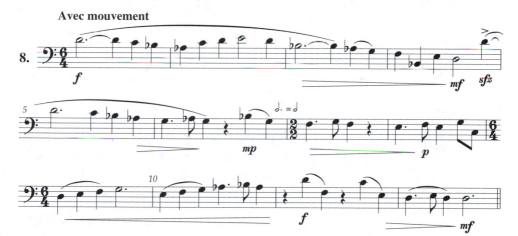

IV. EXCERPTS FROM THE LITERATURE

Traditional Bulgarian, *THE GREY DOVE*

Zart und herzlich

1.

CARSLILE FLOYD, from *SUSANNAH*

2.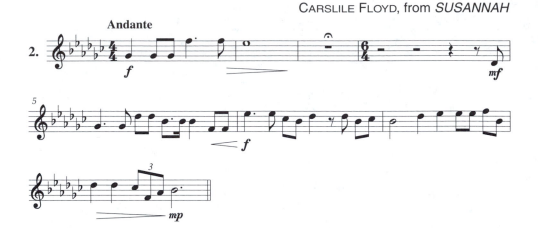

RICHARD WAGNER, from *TRISTAN UND ISOLDE*

3.

MAURICE RAVEL, from *L'HEURE ESPAGNOLE*
(The Spanish Hour)

4.

Claude Debussy, from *PELLEAS ET MÉLISANDE*

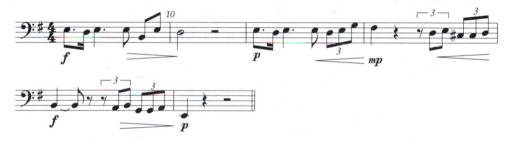

Roger Quilter, from *DREAM VALLEY*

CARL ORFF, *DER MOND*
(The Moon)

CONDUCTUS (13th Century)

V. ENSEMBLES

Suabian Folksong, DOWN IN THE LOWLAND

1.

BÉLA BARTÓK, "From the Island of Bali"
from *MIKROKOSMOS*

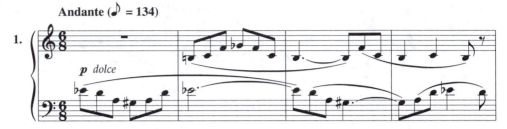

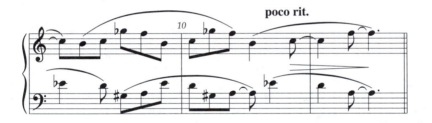

IMOGENE HOLST (Arr.),
THE HEDGES AND FIELDS ARE CLOTHED IN GREEN
(Traditional English Folk Song)

PAUL HINDEMITH, from *MATHIS DER MAHLER*
(Mathis the Painter)

3.

GUILLAUME DUFAY, *RONDEAU* (15th Century)

4.

UNIT NINE

INTERVALLIC SINGING

Alban Berg, *Schliesse Mir Die Augen Biede*

The period 1875–1925 was one of significant change in Western music. While many composers followed the tonal traditions of Brahms and Tchaikovsky well into the twentieth century, others set out in new directions and composed music that was experimental. One such group, known today as the "Second Viennese School," was led by Arnold Schoenberg and his students Anton Webern and Alban Berg.[1] Between about 1913 and 1923, Schoenberg created a new musical system that offered composers a systematic approach to atonal composition. Schoenberg's Twelve-Tone System, termed alternately "serialism," "dodecaphony," and "pantonality," has been influential in the Western world for over three-quarters of a century. More important, perhaps, serialism proved flexible in the hands of later composers who used the system as a springboard for their own innovative styles.

ALBAN BERG (1885–1935) began his work with the harmonic vocabulary of Wagner and Mahler, but quickly embraced the new ideas of his teacher, Arnold Schoenberg. Berg wrote chamber and keyboard works, two operas, a violin concerto, and other compositions that remain in the standard repertory today. In addition to large-scale compositions, however, Berg continued the tradition of the German *lied* as seen here in *Schliesse Mir Die Augen Biede* ("Close My Eyes), a simple song in the style of Schumann, Schubert, and Brahms. Berg wrote the atonal song in 1925—when Serialism was in its infancy—and he constructed it upon a "row," which is an ordering of each of the twelve chromatic pitches.[2] The melody of *Schliesse Mir Die Augen Biede* is strictly serial in that the first pitch, F, is not heard again until each of the other eleven tones has been sounded. The melody is a fivefold statement of the following pitch series (row), on which Berg structured the entire composition.

---

[1] The "first" Viennese school is represented by the eighteenth-century composers Haydn and Mozart.

[2] Serialism is the subject of Chapter 20.

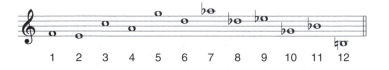

While the pitch content of *Schliesse Mir Die Augen Biede* is unique, the rhythms could be those of Schubert or even Mozart. Still, the melody is atonal; together with the piano accompaniment, the composition presents significant problems for the performer—both in terms of pitch accuracy and interpretation.

ALBAN BERG, *SCHLIESSE MIR DIE AUGEN BIEDE*
(Close My Eyes)

IN UNIT NINE

In CHAPTER 19, you will study atonal and quasi-tonal music, in which an intervallic approach is essential. Even in compositions that are tonal, the melody may roam widely within that context. As a performer, you must decide which measures of a given passage are most easily approached within a tonal framework and which should be sung intervallically. The traditional melodic attractions of $\hat{4}$ to $\hat{3}$ and $\hat{7}$ to $\hat{8}$, after all, serve to verify the mode and tonic pitch respectively. When these attractions are absent, the context of an interval or a group of pitches among its immediate surroundings is more important than such short-term pitch associations in traditional tonal music. In addition, new relationships such as inversion, inclusion, and retrograde are crucial in structuring atonal works.

Also in Chapter 19, you will study mixed meters in which the beat in one meter is *not* equivalent to the beat in the new meter. When $\frac{6}{8}$ changes to $\frac{2}{4}$, for example, the dotted-quarter note may or may not be equivalent to the new quarter-note beat. In the latter case, the metric change is more complex.

Atonal composition in the serial style is the focus of Chapter 20. While singers may not be aware aurally of row permutations in a given melody, a knowledge of the theoretical structure of the composition will surely heighten musical understanding. A detailed discussion of the twelve-tone system is outside the scope of this text, but some of the basic principles will be outlined in Chapter 20. Also included in the chapter are two-part rhythmic studies covering the entire range of traditional rhythmic and metric notation presented in this text.

CHAPTER NINETEEN

Atonal Melodies
Mixed Meters II—Beats Not Equivalent

Allied Theoretical Concepts
- Atonal Theory
- Set Relationships
- Mixed Meter (Beat ≠ Beat)

Concepts in Pitch: Atonal Melody

Composers like Debussy and Bartók created innovative works within the tonal system. At the same time, however, not only did Schoenberg, Webern, and Berg completely reject the principle of tonality after about 1925, but a third group was attracted to styles that might be described as "quasi-tonal." Just what constitutes "atonality," in fact, is open to question.

Atonality

Even before World War I, composers like Charles Ives experimented with compositions where no tonal center could be discerned by the listener. If tonality is defined as a feeling that one pitch is more important than any of the others, then one would expect "atonality" to be defined as the absence of any feeling for key. Such a definition may be too narrow, however, especially in terms of the practical problems associated with performance. ATONALITY is defined here as 1) the absence of a feeling for key, or 2) a sense of key that is created *without* traditional melodic attractions and functional relationships.

In the former category are compositions in which the composer avoided creating a tonal reference. Such works are often highly chromatic, filled with unexpected twists and turns of melody, and/or include dramatic and wide leaps. In other compositions, however the same types of melodic ambiguities will be present, but they will be anchored by at least some semblance of key. The composers of such works avoid traditional scale forms, triad outlines, functional progressions, and melodic attractions, but they achieve a tonal reference in other ways. Accent and repetition are chief among these.

Accent.   As discussed earlier, an accent is a stress placed upon a note or a group of notes.

Metric and agogic accents—employed separately or in combination—can create the sensation of tonality despite a pitch series that is otherwise atonal. In the following melody, the positions of the pitches C, D♭, and B on strong beats center interest on the pitch C despite the lack of melodic tendencies or functional implications and regardless of the fact that the melody ends on the pitch E.

A framework reduction of seemingly atonal passages may reveal relationships such as those in the melody above. Naturally, the concepts of chord and nonchord tones are not applicable. But other means of emphasis, such as accent and embellishment, can be discerned through reduction.

Measure: 1   2   3   4   5   6   7   8

Repetition.   Composers create pockets of tonality through the repetition and/or variation of motives or through the reiteration of individual pitches. The melody below is in G major/minor, but the sense of tonality is created through repetition as opposed to the traditional relationships among diatonic pitches.

Again, a reduction reveals the quasi-tonal relationships inherent in an otherwise ambiguous melody.

Measure: 1   2   3   4   6   7   8

If an atonal melody is highly chromatic, you may find that it has a tonal basis that can be isolated and employed for practice in a simplified version. The melody below, for example, can be reduced to a framework that has clear tonal implications.

Reduction

While whole-tone melodies are not necessarily atonal, they lack traditional melodic tendencies and may feature augmented triad outlines. In addition to reduction, you may find it helpful at first to practice atonal or quasi-tonal melodies in fragments. Study the melody, for example, and determine where three or four pitches lie in familiar diatonic patterns. As shown below, instead of viewing the entire line as a series of abstract intervals, use one interval as a link between two well-known patterns. The passage will thus become a mosaic of familiar scales, modes, or triad fragments connected by familiar intervals. While such a segmentation will facilitate singing, however, remember that the composer probably did not conceive the music in bite-sized pieces. When you can sing the composition accurately, adhere closely to the composer's phrasing and other performance instructions to create a musical whole.

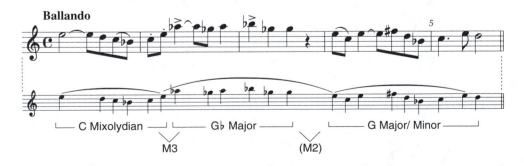

RELATIONSHIPS IN ATONAL MELODY

While some twentieth-century melodies are quasi-tonal, others are unabashedly atonal. Without traditional melodic tendencies that help the listener grasp the tonal goal of a given passage, atonal composers employ other relationships that lend structure. These relationships may be either ordered or unordered, but the concept of PITCH CLASS is central to both.

Pitch Class.   As discussed earlier, traditional composers never notated a pitch capriciously. In Bach, Mozart, or Verdi, the pitch A♯ tends to move to B; likewise, B♭ descends naturally to A. In atonal music however, notation is typically one of convenience and dependent entirely upon pitch class.

A pitch class is one tone of the chromatic scale together with all of its enharmonic and octave duplications. The pitches C, B♯, and D♭♭, for example, are all in the same pitch class. Likewise, F♯, G♭, and E× share a single pitch class. In atonal music, double sharps and double flats are avoided; otherwise, any pitch in a given pitch class is appropriate.

Same Pitch Class   Different Pitch Classes

Pitch class is important in understanding the concepts of inversion, transposition, retrograde, and complementation. These concepts will be discussed as related to the following fragment comprised of six different pitch classes.

Ordered Relationships

Several relationships in atonal music depend upon the retention of the original order of pitches in a given set. These include inversion, transposition, retrograde, and retrograde inversion.

Inversion.   MIRROR INVERSION is the process of duplicating a set of notes by the same intervals, but in the opposite direction. In the passage below, the original set begins the phrase while the literal mirror inversion ends it.

Transposition.   Sets need not be sounded at the original pitch level to be heard as clearly related. The transposition of an original pattern or any other transformation of the set is a common structural element in atonal works. The original pitch series is transformed here through a transposition (M2 higher) and a transposed inversion (P5 higher).

Retrograde.   A pattern heard backward—either transposed or at the original tonal level—is another method of lending structure and substance to an atonal work. Any transformation of a set can be stated in RETROGRADE or backward form. The phrase below, for example, is a transformation of the original set heard first in pure retrograde form and next in a transposed RETRO-GRADE INVERSION (the inverted form stated backward).

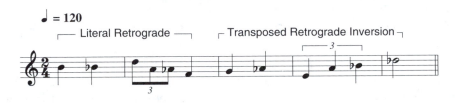

Unordered Relationships

Two important relationships, complementation and inclusion, depend upon content rather than order. As with other relationships, any notation within a given pitch class is appropriate (although double sharps and flats are generally avoided).

Complementation.   The COMPLEMENT of a given set of notes is comprised of all notes not in the original set. The complement of a C major scale, for example, is a set comprised of all pitches *not* included in the C major scale.

Set   Complement

Composers of atonal music sometimes use a given set in the melody and the complement of that set as an accompaniment. Alternately, the literal or transposed complement of a melodic fragment may follow the fragment itself.

Inclusion

A final unordered relationship common in atonal music is that of *inclusion*. The INCLUSION relation involves a subset that is present within a given set of notes. The three subsets below (A, B, and C) are all related to the original set through inclusion. The first (A) is literal; the second and third (B and C) are transposed. Notice that order is not a factor in the inclusion relation.

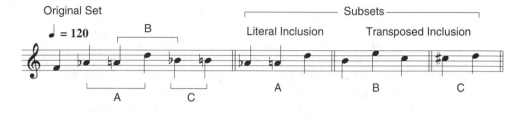

Concepts in Rhythm: Mixed Meter II

If a composer changes from $\frac{2}{4}$ to $\frac{6}{8}$, two possibilities exist: the quarter note and dotted-quarter note have the same value in time (♩ = ♩.), or the *eighth notes* in the two meters are equivalent (♪ = ♪). In the first passage below, the speed of the beat remains the same. In the second passage, the beat slows by one-half.

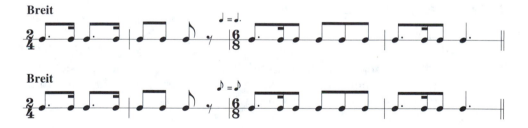

In the second of the two lines above, notice that while the beats are not equal, the *eighth notes* are. To practice the passage, set a metronome at the eighth-note pulse and use this as a guide when meters change. Overemphasize accents at first to clarify the metric changes.

Other metric changes can be approached in a similar way. While the beats in $\frac{6}{4}$ and $\frac{2}{2}$ are not equal, for example, the quarter notes will be.

Unless otherwise noted, beats in mixed meters should be considered equivalent.

Measured Rhythm

A CADENZA is a passage in an instrumental concerto for the soloist alone. MEASURED RHYTHM, which is often employed in cadenzas, is based on fractional values, but typically has no metric structure. Passages in measured rhythm are often written with neither meter signature nor barlines. Some composers of vocal music have also employed measured rhythm to create an improvisatory effect for all or part of a work. In the passage below, the note values are provided, but without barlines. Unless indicated by the composer or an editor, accents are determined by the performer (with beaming as a guide).

RHYTHMIC READING

I. WARM-UPS

Before performance, study the lines below to determine the structure of any mixed meters. Use counting syllables, a single pitch, or another method recommended by your instructor.

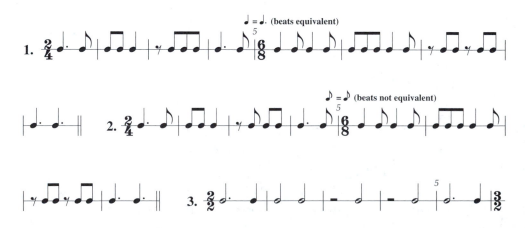

The following warm-ups may be performed as two-part studies.

II. EXERCISES

The composition below is a "theme" with two variations. Begin by analyzing the music and adding performance instructions *in English*. Next, study the rhythmic material of the theme and be prepared to discuss it in terms of rhythmic and motivic use, form, variety, and so on. Finally, conduct a similar analysis on each of the two variations.

Composition.   Compose melodies based on the rhythmic theme and both of the variations given in the previous analysis exercise. The theme might be in a major key, for example, the first variation in Phrygian mode, and the second variation could be atonal. Three of the many additional possibilities for melodic structure are suggested below.

Theme	Variation I	Variation II
Dorian	Lydian	Aeolian
Synthetic	Pentatonic	Atonal
Major	Atonal	Quartal

Complete the composition by adding tempo and performance instructions that are either the same or different from those that you were asked to provide originally.

SIGHT SINGING

I. WARM-UPS

Study the warm-up passages below. Most are atonal, but many of them include fragments of familiar melodic or harmonic materials. Make a reduction of the passages that emphasizes various accents, motives, and so on. Look also for transformations of a basic set and be prepared to identify and classify relationships as appropriate.

II. EXERCISES

The following melodies are atonal or have only fleeting tonal implications. First, add tempo and performance instructions *in Italian*. Next, analyze each melody for any familiar melodic or harmonic patterns. Locate points of tonal reference including repetition and accent.

Composition.   Accustomed as we are to traditional tonal music, composing a well-organized atonal melody may be daunting. Begin by selecting a formal plan for a melody of approximately sixteen measures (thirty-two measures if you choose a two-beat meter). Next, devise several atonal sets of five or six pitches. Choose two or three of those that you feel have the greatest potential and notate a number of different transformations of each set. Use the suggested list of transformations below or choose others that you feel best exhibit the characteristics of the original sets.

    a. Transposition a major third higher
    b. The literal inversion
    c. The inversion transposed down a minor second
    d. The literal retrograde
    e. The retrograde transposed up a perfect fourth
    f. The complement of the original motive
    g. Two different sets included within the original motive

Write a complete atonal melody based on the original set and one or more of its transformations. The rhythms that you apply to the various transformations should not be random, but rather clearly related to the original material. To insure an interesting and structurally effective rhythm, you might begin the melody by composing a rhythmic solo, then applying the pitches of the melody to the rhythms. You might also assume the rhythms of a study from this or another chapter as the basis of the melody.

III. STUDIES

Andantino

2.

Bewegt

3.

Scherzando

4.

IV. EXCERPTS FROM THE LITERATURE

ARNOLD SCHOENBERG, *PIERROT LUNAIRE,* "Valse de Chopin"

Langsamer waltzer

CHARLES IVES, *THE CAGE*

ALBAN BERG, Four Songs (Number 3)

Erst ziemlich bewegt, dann langsam

MARC SATTERWHITE, from *PAINTING FOR THE BLIND*

p sempre legato

V. ENSEMBLES

JAMES MOBBERLEY, Trio

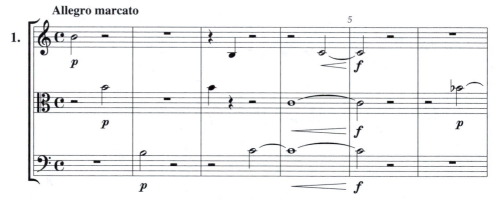

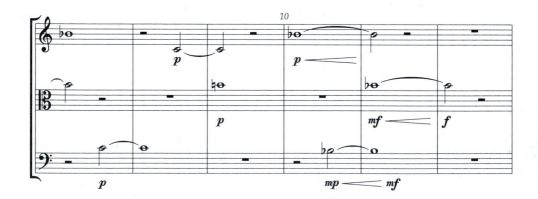

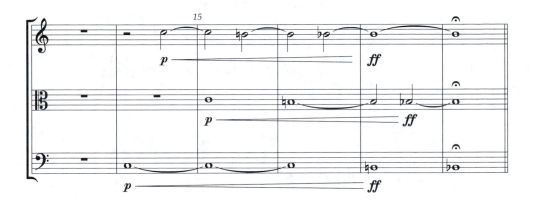

IGOR STRAVINSKY, from *THRENI*

CHAPTER TWENTY

Serialism
Review of Two-Part Studies

Allied Theoretical Concepts
- Serialism
- The Row and its Transformations

Concepts in Pitch: Serialism

Composers who turned to atonal composition in the early twentieth century sometimes found organization problematic. Without traditional key relationships, for example, listeners were less able to follow the formal progress of a longer work. Likewise, for composers trained in the theory of traditional music, *assuring* atonality was no simple task. Clearly, some method of organizing atonal music was necessary if this new approach was to reach its full potential.

Arnold Schoenberg devised the Twelve-Tone Serial technique. Schoenberg began his work in a tonal style similar to that of Claude Debussy, embraced atonality about 1910, and had completed several important compositions using this approach by 1913. He produced no new compositions until 1923, however. During this ten year period he developed and explored the potential of a completely new music. Together with his principal students, Webern and Berg, Schoenberg created a new way of composing that assured both atonality and effective organization.

THE TWELVE-TONE METHOD

Composers of twelve-tone (serial) music begin with a ROW. A row is an ordering of each of the twelve chromatic pitches. Rows are not composed randomly, but typically have some organizing feature such as the predominance of a certain type of interval (a major sixth, perhaps), a balance of ascending and descending intervals, or other symmetrical structure. The row that Alban Berg composed for his *Schliesse Mir Die Augen Biede,* although vocally conceived, includes wide leaps, a combination of consonant and dissonant intervals, and an arch-like contour.

When you study the entire melody of *Schliesse Mir Die Augen Biede* (page 318), you will see that the row is stated five times in its literal form. Each statement begins with the pitch F and ends with the pitch B. While the rhythms change for each statement of the row, the order of the twelve pitches is maintained.

Transformations of the Row

While Berg used only the original row in the melody, several transformations are commonly employed by serial composers. These are the same transformations discussed in Chapter 19 in association with a set: Transposition, Retrograde, Inversion, and Retrograde Inversion.

Transposition.   The original or "prime" form of the row (designated "P^0") can be transposed to eleven additional pitch levels. The designation of transposed row forms indicates the number of half steps between the transposition and the original row. In the case of the Berg row, a transposition three half steps higher begins on A♭ or G♯ and is designated "P^3"; a transposition ten half steps higher (P^{10}) begins on E♭ or D♯.[1]

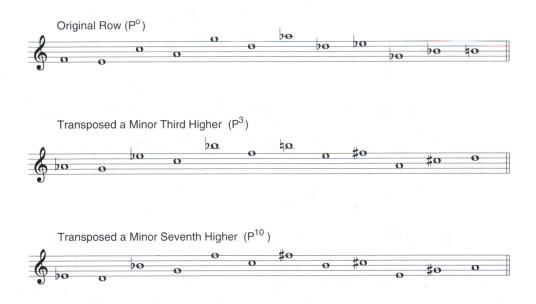

Original Row (P^0)

Transposed a Minor Third Higher (P^3)

Transposed a Minor Seventh Higher (P^{10})

[1]Because transpositions ten half steps higher and two half steps lower produce the same pitches, the notation of "P^{10}" is not exceptional. In the most strict sense, octave placement is not a factor in determining row transformations.

Remember that in atonal music there are few rules for "correct" spelling. Composers avoid double flats and double sharps, but otherwise, an A♯ is just as correct as a B♭. In your own vocal compositions, however, you would be well advised to notate intervals simply. While the sounds are the same, a doubly augmented fourth *looks* more difficult than a perfect fifth.

Retrograde.   The RETROGRADE, the original row stated backward, is designated "R⁰." The retrograde versions of the three prime forms above are identified as R^0, R^3, and R^{10} respectively.

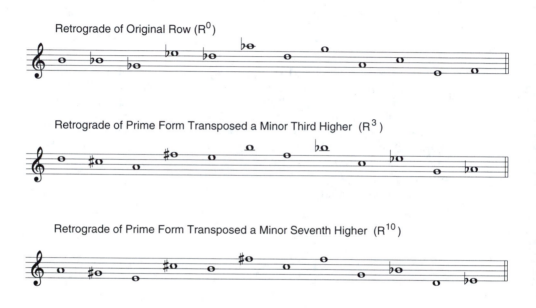

Retrograde of Original Row (R^0)

Retrograde of Prime Form Transposed a Minor Third Higher (R^3)

Retrograde of Prime Form Transposed a Minor Seventh Higher (R^{10})

Inversion. The term "inversion" in twelve-tone terminology refers to a *mirror* inversion. Beginning with the first pitch in the prime form, the INVERSION is created by duplicating the intervals in the opposite direction. The inversion of the original row (I^0), for example, is given below.

Inversion of Original Row (I^0)

Like transpositions of the prime, transposed inversions of the row are designated according to the interval of transposition stated in half steps. The literal inversion is I^0; the inversion transposed a minor third (three half steps) higher is I^3, and so on.

Inversion of Prime Form Transposed a Minor Third Higher (I^3)

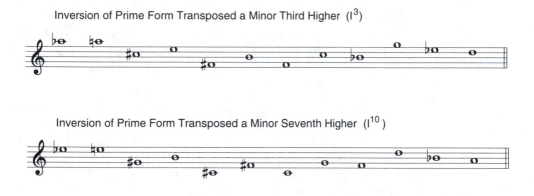

Inversion of Prime Form Transposed a Minor Seventh Higher (I^{10})

Retrograde Inversion. A final transformation of the row is the reverse form of the inversion, or the RETROGRADE INVERSION.

Retrograde Inversion of Original Row (RI^0)

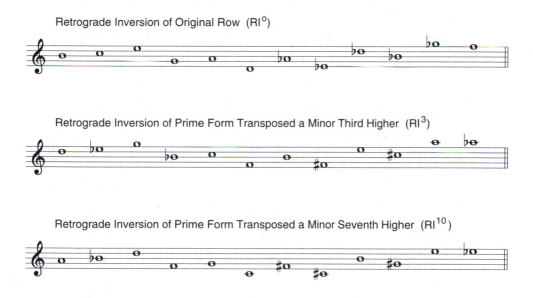

Retrograde Inversion of Prime Form Transposed a Minor Third Higher (RI^3)

Retrograde Inversion of Prime Form Transposed a Minor Seventh Higher (RI^{10})

Singing Serial Melodies

Unless you have absolute pitch, singing atonal melodies—whether serial or not—is challenging. In addition to suggestions from your instructor, follow the procedures discussed elsewhere in this text and summarized below.

a. Analyze the melody to determine its structure.
b. If the melody is atonal, locate passages that outline familiar materials, such as triads or scales.
c. Locate any recurring pitches that may anchor a longer melodic fragment (this will not occur in strict serial compositions).
d. If the composition is serial, identify row forms used in the melody.
e. Practice at the keyboard, check your pitch often, and work on the melody alone before moving on to a full performance with rhythm and expression.

Study the melody of Berg's *Schliesse Mir Die Augen Biede* and notice that while the initial statement of the row is atonal and contains wide leaps, it can be viewed in two tonal fragments connected by a tritone and ending with a half step. The first fragment may be viewed in F major; the second, in C♭ major. While the accents and phrasing of the melody do not support the tonal analysis (not to mention the atonal piano accompaniment), this approach may be useful for analysis and practice. In actual performance, however, the piano accompaniment will contradict the tonal implications of the melody.

Naturally, all serial melodies are not so easily associated with tonal materials as is the Berg song. On the other hand, even the most disjunct and seemingly irregular melodies are not typically merely successions of abstract intervals. In Schoenberg's brief song, *Tot* ("Death"), for example, few familiar patterns are apparent at first glance.

ARNOLD SCHOENBERG, *TOT*

You might find it useful to eliminate the pitch A in measure 1 and practice the fragment first as an embellished minor seventh. When the pitch A is restored, the tritone, sandwiched between two familiar tones, should be less difficult.

Likewise, the melodic fragment in measure 2 can be heard in F minor.

The second half of the row can be practiced in C major ending on raised 4̂.

Compound Intervals.   Berg's *Schliesse Mir Die Augen Biede* features wide intervals including ninths, tenths, and even an eleventh. As discussed earlier, begin by reducing the compound interval by an octave. While the leaps in the first six pitches of Berg's melody are conveniently heard in F major, the fourth measure includes a diminished octave, a diminished twelfth, and a major tenth.

Practice this passage at first with all of the tones in the same octave as shown below. When you become familiar with the sound of the basic intervals, restore the octave leaps one by one until you are singing the passage as written.

Concepts in Rhythm: Review of Two-Part Studies

This final rhythmic reading section centers on two-part studies involving problems already introduced. Approach the problems as you have in previous chapters (see page 189).

RHYTHMIC READING

I. WARM-UPS

1.

2.

3.
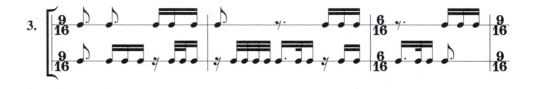

4.

5.

6.
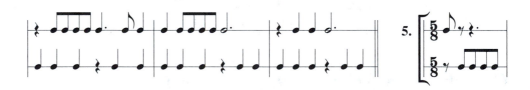

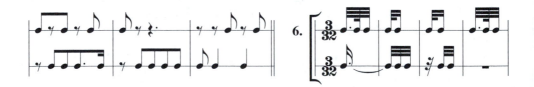

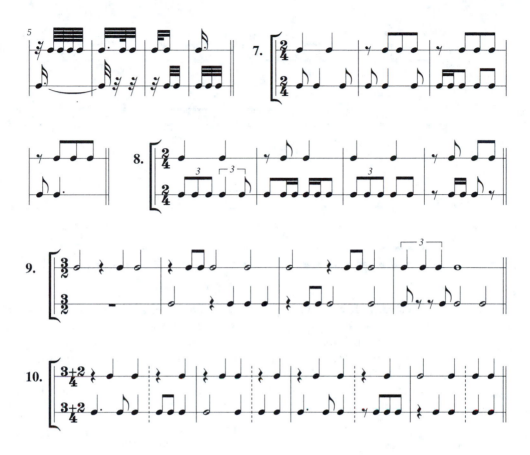

II. EXERCISES

Analysis. Study the rhythmic and metric structure of the two solos below. First add tempo and performance instructions in the language of your choice. Next conduct a detailed analysis of both solos and be prepared to compare them in terms of type(s) of rhythm employed, metric structure, use of rhythmic devices such as syncopation, motivic use and development, and formal plan. If directed to do so, write a brief paper detailing the results of your analyses.

Composition. Compose a percussion ensemble for four to six performers. Use either standard percussion instruments or instruments that you conceive and construct yourself. At least one instrument should be capable of two or more different (indefinite) pitches. Structure your composition either as a suite of three related movements or as a continuous work in binary (A B) or ternary (A B A) form. As directed, include some or all of the following in your composition.

   a. A brief cadenza for one instrument that is notated in measured rhythm.
   b. A passage in which instrument entries are staggered (every four beats, every two measures, and so on). You might also write parts that have staggered silences.
   c. Include a metric change in which beats in the two meters are not equal.
   d. Employ two-against-three in which the borrowed division in one part is contrasted with the natural division in one or more others.
   e. An extended duet for two of your instruments.

SIGHT SINGING

I. WARM-UPS

The warm-ups that follow are all transformations of the row shown below. Your instructor may want you to make a matrix for this row and determine the structure of each warm-up.

II. EXERCISES

Determine the twelve-tone row that is the basis of the following two melodies. Make a matrix for this row that shows all forty-eight forms. Analyze the row and be prepared to comment on its internal structure.

Composition. Compose a twelve-tone row that is based on one of the following structures (or another recommended by your instructor):

a. A preponderance of perfect fourths.
b. A trichord that is inverted for pitches 4–6 and transposed for pitches 7–9. The three remaining pitches will constitute the final trichord.
c. A row that has whole-tone characteristics (a whole tone scale transposed a minor second higher includes all twelve pitches).
d. A row based on a succession of major and/or minor triads. When no more triads are possible without repeating pitches, order the remaining pitches as you deem appropriate.
e. A hexachord that, when inverted, yields the other six pitches of the chromatic scale.

Make a matrix of your row and study the possibilities for sequential combination. Choose two or three different row transformations and employ them, along with the prime form, in the composition of a complete melody. Remember that when tonality is absent, you will need to impart continuity and contrast through other means (rhythmic structure, form, and so on). You may want to begin, for example, with a complete formal plan and/or with a rhythmic solo to which you will then apply the pitches of the row. Once again, remember that you may repeat any given pitch of the row as many times as you want to before moving on to the next pitch. Complete the composition with tempo and other instructions in English.

III. STUDIES

The following studies are all based upon the same twelve-tone row that is stated in the first melody. Various transformations of the row are employed in other studies.

Some employ a loose serial technique with the repetition of cells, the overlapping of row forms, and so on.

Briskly

1.

Moderato

2.

sotto voce

Kräftig

3.

Mässig und ausdrucksvoll

Allegro non troppo

Schnell

IV. *EXCERPTS FROM THE LITERATURE*

ARNOLD SCHOENBERG, *TOT*
(Death)

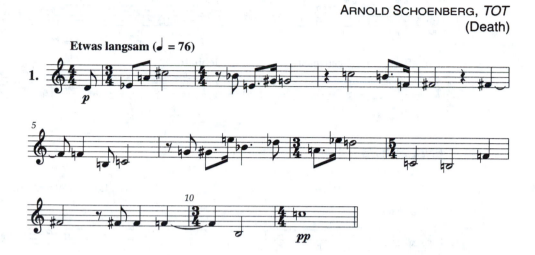

LUIGI DALLAPICCOLA, *CINQUE CANTI* (I)
(Five Songs)

ANTON WEBERN, from Cantata, Op. 29

V. ENSEMBLES

CARL PANDOLFI, Duet

MILTON BABBITT, Duet

Glossary of Foreign Terms

Terms are Italian unless identified otherwise.

À (Fr.) To.

Aber (Gr.) But.

Accelerando Increasing speed.

Adagietto Somewhat faster than *Adagio*.

Adagio Moderately slow tempo.

Affekt (Gr.) With affection, emotion.

Affetuoso Tender.

Agitato Agitated.

Al To the.

Alla In the manner of.

Allargando Slowing in tempo.

Allegretto Slightly slower than *Allegro*.

Allegro A relatively fast tempo.

Amabile Lovingly.

Amaroso Lovingly.

Andante Walking tempo. A natural pace.

Andantino Somewhat faster than *Andante*.

Animato Animated.

Animé (Fr.) Animated.

Anmutig (Gr.) Graceful.

Ansdrucksvoll (Gr.) Expressive.

Assez (Fr.) Somewhat, fairly.

Avec (Fr.) With.

Ballando Dancing.

Ben Well, rather.

Bewegt (Gr.) Agitated.

Breit (Gr.) Bright, cheerful.

Brillante With brillance.

Brio Spirit.

Caesura Break, silence (//).

Calando Lessening in dynamics and tempo.

Calore Warmth.

Cantabile In a singing style.

Cédez (Fr.) Becoming slower.

Coda Concluding passage (⊕).

Commodo Quiet, calm.

Crescendo Gradually increasing in volume.

Dann (Gr.) Then.

Deciso Decisively.

Decrescendo Gradually lessening in volume.

Deliberato With deliberation.

Deutlich (Gr.) Clear, precise.

Divisi Divided, divide.

Doch (Gr.) Still.

Dolce Sweetly.

Doucement (Fr.) Sweet.

Dur (Gr.) Major.

E And/then.

Ed And/then (used before vowels).

Einfach (Gr.) Simple, easy.

Empfundung (Gr.) Expression.

En Allant (Fr.) Flowing, going (as in *Andante*).

Energico Energetic.

Erst (Gr.) First.

Et (Fr.) And.

Etude Study.

Etwas (Gr.) Somewhat.

Expressif (Fr.) Expressive.

Expressione Expression.

Fantasia Fantasy, with whimsy.

Feierlich (Gr.) Solemn.

Fermata Pause (⌢).

Feroce   Fiercely, with ferocity.

Fine   (The) end.

Fliessand   (Gr.) Flowing.

Forza   With strength, force.

Fretta   Haste, quickness.

Frisch   (Gr.) Brisk.

Fröhlich   Gay.

Fuoco   Fire.

Gai   (Fr.) Lively.

Gehend   (Gr.) A walking pace (as in *Andante*).

Gemächlich   (Gr.) Easy, comfortable.

Geshwind   (Gr.) Quick, lively.

Getragen   (Gr.) Sustained.

Giacoso   Playful.

Gioviale   Jovial.

Gracieux   (Fr.) Graceful.

Grazioso   Graceful.

Grave   Quite slow.

Graziös   (Gr.) Graceful.

Heiter   (Gr.) Cheerful.

Herzlich   (Gr.) Heartfelt.

Immer   (Gr.) Always.

Innig   (Gr.) Ardent.

Klar   (Gr.) Clear.

Kraft   (Gr.) Strength.

Kräftig   (Gr.) Strong.

Langsam   (Gr.) Slow.

Largando   Becoming slower and broader.

Larghetto   Slightly faster than Largo.

Largo   Slow and broad.

Lebhaft   (Gr.) Lively, animated.

Léger   (Fr.) Light.

Leicht   (Gr.) Easy, light.

Leiden   (Gr.) Sorrow.

Lent   (Fr.) Slow.

Lentement   (Fr.) Slowly.

Lenteur   (Fr.) Slow(ness), ritarding.

Lento   Slow, but faster than Adagio.

L'istesso   The same (as in L'istesso tempo).

Lunga   Long.

Lustig   (Gr.) Happy and gay.

Ma   But.

Maestoso   Majestic.

Maggiore   Major.

Majeur   (Fr.) Major.

Marcato   Marked, emphasized.

Marcia   March.

Marziale   Martial, military style.

Mässig   (Gr.) Moderate tempo.

Mehr   (Gr.) More.

Meno   Less.

Mesto   Sad, mournful.

Mineur   (Fr.) Minor.

Minore   Minor.

Mit   (Gr.) With.

Moderato   A moderate tempo. Slower than *allegro*.

Modéré   (Fr.) Moderate.

Moll   (Gr.) Minor.

Molto   Much.

Morendo   Dying away.

Mosso   Tempo, motion.

Mouvement   (Fr.) Movement.

Nicht   (Gr.) Not.

Non   (Fr.) Not.

Ohne   (Gr.) Without.

Pendendosi   Gradually dying away.

Peu   (Fr.) Little.

Piacevole   Pleasant, in grace.

Più   More.

Plus   (Fr.) More.

Poco   A little, slightly.

Pressanso   Moving forward.

Pressez   (Fr.) Pressing forward.

Presto   Quite fast.

Primo   First.

Rallentando   Gradually slowing.

Rasch   (Gr.) Fast.

Retenu   (Fr.) Held back.

Ritardando   Gradually slowing.

Ritenuto   More slowly.

Ritmoco   Rhythmically. With a clearly marked rhythm.

Rubato   Pushing or pulling in tempo.

Ruhig   (Gr.) Quietly.

Salterello   An Italian dance with a marked "jumping" movement.

Sans   (Fr.) Without.

Scherzando   Light and playful.

Schnell   (Gr.) Quick.

Sehr   (Gr.) Very.

Semplice   Simple, unaffected.

Sempre   Always, constantly.

Sentimentale   With emotion, affect.

Segno   Sign (𝄋).

Senza   Without.

Siciliano   Slow dance in compound meter.

Sostenuto   Sustained.

Sotto   Under.

Sotto Voce   Undertone, quietly.

Spiritoso   With spirit, agitated.

Stentando   Slowing.

Stringendo   Growing faster in tempo.

Subito   Suddenly.

Tanto   So much, as.

Tarantella   Fast dance in compound meter.

Tempo di Valse   A waltz tempo or medium three-beat pulse.

Tempo   Time, the beat.

Tempo Primo   The initial tempo.

Teneramente   Tenderly.

Timoroso   Hesitant, timid.

Tranquillo   Tranquil.

Trés   (Fr.) Very.

Tristezza   Sadness, sorrow.

Trop   Too, as.

Troppo   Too, too much.

Tutti   All.

Und   (Gr.) And.

Valse   (Fr.) A waltz tempo.

Vif   (Fr.) Lively.

Vite   (Fr.) Quickly.

Vivace   Lively, quickly.

Vivo   Lively, animated.

Voce   Voice.

Vortragen   (Gr.) To play, perform.

Walzer   (Gr.) Waltz.

Wieder   (Gr.) Against, contrary to.

Zart   (Gr.) Soft and tender.

Ziemlich   (Gr.) Somewhat.

Zu   (Gr.) Too.

Zurückhalten   (Gr.) Hold back, retard.

Common Symbols
and Abbreviations

ABBREVIATIONS

D. C.	**Da Capo** (the head, beginning). Return to the beginning.
D. C. al Fine	Return to the beginning; conclude with the measure marked "fine."
D. S.	**Dal Segno** (the sign). Return to the sign (𝄋).
D. S. al Fine	Return to the sign; conclude with the measure marked "fine."
G. P.	**Grand** (General) **Pause.** A complete and substantial silence.

SIGNS AND SYMBOLS

//	**Caesura**	A relatively lengthy silence (sufficient to break the flow of beats).
⊕	**Coda**	Repeat from the beginning. Go to the coda at the sign.
◁	**Crescendo**	Gradual increase in volume.
▷	**Decrescendo**	Gradual decrease in volume.
⌒	**Fermata**	A relative lengthening of a note or rest (sufficient to break the flow of beats).
1.	**First Ending**	Used with repeated material. Perform this material the first time.
‖: :‖	**Repeat**	Play the material within the double bars a second time.
,	**Short Pause**	Usually an indication of phrasing or breathing.
2.	**Second Ending**	Used with repeated material. Skip the first ending; play the material in the second ending measure(s).
𝄋	**Segno**	"The Sign." Marks a point in the music for repetition.

Index

Credits